Beagle

2nd Edition

GET MORE!
Visit www.wiley.com/
go/beagle

Elaine Waldorf Gewirtz

Howell
Book House™

The publisher and the author make no representations or warranties with respect to the accuracy or completeness of the contents of this work and specifically disclaim all warranties, including without limitation warranties of fitness for a particular purpose. No warranty may be created or extended by sales or promotional materials. The advice and strategies contained herein may not be suitable for every situation. This work is sold with the understanding that the publisher is not engaged in rendering legal, accounting, or other professional services. If professional assistance is required, the services of a competent professional person should be sought. Neither the publisher nor the author shall be liable for damages arising here from. The fact that an organization or Website is referred to in this work as a citation and/or a potential source of further information does not mean that the author or the publisher endorses the information the organization or Website may provide or recommendations it may make. Further, readers should be aware that Internet Websites listed in this work may have changed or disappeared between when this work was written and when it is read.

For general information on our other products and services or to obtain technical support please contact our Customer Care Department within the U.S. at (800) 762-2974, outside the U.S. at (317) 572-3993 or fax (317) 572-4002.

Wiley also publishes its books in a variety of electronic formats. Some content that appears in print may not be available in electronic books. For more information about Wiley products, please visit our web site at www.wiley.com.

ISBN 978-0-470-39055-9

Printed in the United States of America

10 9 8 7 6 5 4 3 2 1

2nd Edition

Book design by Melissa Auciello-Brogan
Cover design by Michael J. Freeland
Illustrations in chapter 9 by Shelley Norris and Karl Brandt
Book production by Wiley Publishing, Inc. Composition Services

About the Author

Elaine Waldorf Gewirtz is the author of several books about dogs, including *Pugs For Dummies, Boston Terrier: Your Happy Healthy Pet* (2nd Edition), *Chihuahua: Your Happy Healthy Pet* (2nd Edition), and *Miniature Schnauzer: Your Happy Healthy Pet* (2nd Edition). She is a multiple winner of the Dog Writers Association of America's Maxwell Award for Excellence and the recipient of the Hartz Mountain Award and the ASPCA's Special Writing Award.

Elaine is a member of the Dog Writers Association of America, the American Society of Journalists and Authors, and the Independent Writers of Southern California. She shows and breeds Dalmatians in conformation and has lived with several breeds all her life.

About Howell Book House

Since 1961, Howell Book House has been America's premier publisher of pet books. We're dedicated to companion animals and the people who love them, and our books reflect that commitment. Our stable of authors—training experts, veterinarians, breeders, and other authorities—is second to none. And we've won more Maxwell Awards from the Dog Writers Association of America than any other publisher.

As we head toward the half-century mark, we're more committed than ever to providing new and innovative books, along with the classics our readers have grown to love. From bringing home a new puppy to competing in advanced equestrian events, Howell has the titles that keep animal lovers coming back again and again.

Contents

Shopping List

You'll need to do a bit of stocking up before you bring your new dog or puppy home. Below is a basic list of some must-have supplies. For more detailed information on the selection of each item below, consult chapter 5. For specific guidance on what grooming tools you'll need, review chapter 7.

- ☐ Stainless steel food dish
- ☐ Stainless steel water dish
- ☐ Dog food
- ☐ Leash
- ☐ Collar
- ☐ Crate
- ☐ Nail clippers

- ☐ Grooming tools (bristle brush, shedding blade, flea comb)
- ☐ Chew toys
- ☐ Toys
- ☐ Flea, tick, and heartworm preventives
- ☐ Enzymatic cleaning products
- ☐ ID tag and microchip

There are likely to be a few other items that you're dying to pick up before bringing your dog home. Use the following blanks to note any additional items you'll be shopping for.

- ☐ _____
- ☐ _____
- ☐ _____
- ☐ _____
- ☐ _____
- ☐ _____
- ☐ _____
- ☐ _____
- ☐ _____
- ☐ _____
- ☐ _____
- ☐ _____

Pet Sitter's Guide

We can be reached at (__)_____-_____ Cell phone (__)_____-_____

We will return on _____ (date) at _____ (approximate time)

Dog's Name _____

Breed, Age, and Sex _____

Spayed or neutered? _____

Date last heartworm preventive given _____

Date last flea and tick preventive given _____

Important Names and Numbers

Vet's Name _____ Phone (__)_____- _____

Address _____

Emergency Vet's Name _____ Phone (__)_____- _____

Address _____

Poison Control _____ (or call vet first)

Other individual to contact in case of emergency _____

_____

Care Instructions

In the following blanks, let the pet sitter know what to feed, how much, and when; when the dog should go out; when to give treats; and when to exercise the dog.

Morning _____

_____

Afternoon _____

_____

Evening _____

_____

Medications needed (dosage and schedule) _____

_____

Any special medical conditions _____

_____

Grooming instructions _____

_____

My dog's favorite playtime activities, quirks, and other tips _____

_____

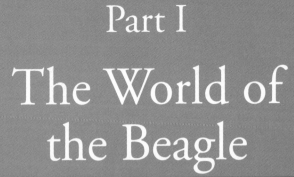

Part I
The World of the Beagle

The Beagle

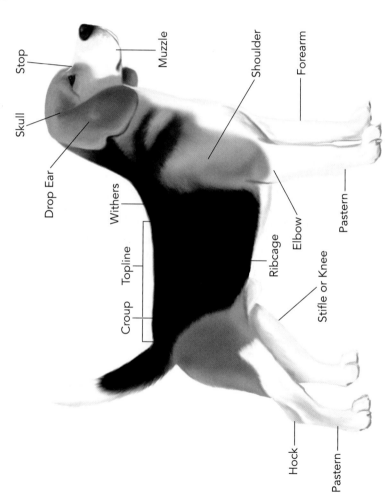

Stop

Skull

Drop Ear

Muzzle

Withers

Topline

Croup

Shoulder

Forearm

Ribcage

Elbow

Pastern

Stifle or Knee

Hock

Pastern

Chapter 1

What Is a Beagle?

Dream big. That's what Snoopy, one of America's best-loved icons, liked to think. Snoopy was Joe Cool, World War I Flying Ace, Big Man on Campus, Literary Agent, Flashbeagle, and Foreign Legionnaire. There wasn't any persona this extroverted Beagle with the overactive imagination couldn't assume. Snoopy was cartoonist Charles M. Schulz's lifelong muse.

Although it's difficult to imagine this marshmallow of a cartoon canine running after rabbits—or anything else for that matter—Snoopy's intelligence and quick wit embraces the spirit of all Beagles the world over: enterprising, mischievous, and downright cuddly loveable.

Apparently, everyone agrees. From 1953 through 1959, the Beagle was the top dog among all breeds registered by the AKC, and the breed has ranked either fourth, fifth, or sixth ever since. Certainly, the Beagle is one Joe Cool dog.

Something Like a Hound Dog

The Beagle is a hound, a scenthound to be exact, who hunts prey primarily by scent. A member of a select fraternity within the canine world, the Beagle was originally bred to hunt as part of a large pack.

First and foremost, a Beagle is a scenthound who hunts with his nose.

He is the little cousin of the Foxhound, who is depicted in paintings of horses and hounds in the English countryside. He is also the more active, less melancholic cousin of the Basset Hound. Like the Basset, the Beagle's primary quarry is the hare or rabbit.

The little puppy asleep on your lap may not know all of this, but it's important for you to know this, because it will help you understand this marvelous little creature.

How the Beagle's mind works, why he acts the way he does, and why he looks the way he does isn't a big mystery. The more you know about your little hound, the easier it is to keep him healthy, happy, and very well adjusted.

The Ideal Beagle

The perfect Beagle is probably already taking a nap in your house, and chances are you don't care whether he is taller than fifteen inches, his coat is thin, or he's long and lean. All that matters to you is the way he looks up at you with love in his eyes and follows you from room to room.

All Beagles have that natural appeal and an inner beauty all their own. If you read the official breed standard for the Beagle though, the ideal hound needs to have more than the look of love. By working hard to meet the standard, breeders try to produce the best Beagles they can.

In this chapter, you'll find a basic description of the Beagle, as set out by the breed standard. If you're wondering if your Beagle fits the standard, give it a read. You can also ask your dog's breeder. Most responsible breeders are true Beagle experts and are happy to share what they have learned over the years with a new owner, both for your benefit and for the good of your puppy. Your veterinarian can usually let you know if anything structural is amiss with your dog.

What Is a Breed Standard?

A breed standard is a detailed description of the perfect dog of that breed. Breeders use the standard as a guide in their breeding programs, and judges use it to evaluate the dogs in conformation shows. The standard is written by the national breed club, using guidelines established by the registry that recognizes the breed (such as the AKC or UKC).

Usually, the first section of the breed standard gives a brief overview of the breed's history. Then it describes the dog's general appearance and size as an adult. Next is a detailed description of the head and neck, then the back and body, and the front and rear legs. The standard then describes the ideal coat and how the dog should be presented in the show ring. It also lists all acceptable colors, patterns, and markings. Then there's a section on how the dog moves, called *gait*. Finally, there's a general description of the dog's temperament.

Each section also lists characteristics that are considered to be faults or disqualifications in the conformation ring. Superficial faults in appearance are often what distinguish a pet-quality dog from a show- or competition-quality dog. However, some faults affect the way a dog moves or his overall health. And faults in temperament are serious business. You can read all the AKC breed standards at www.akc.org.

Overall Appearance

A miniature Foxhound, the Beagle should be big and solid in relation to his height, and look like a dog who can go the distance in the chase to follow his quarry until the end. This description applies to the field dog as well as the show Beagle.

He should be nicely proportioned and built squarely, with a straight back. This overall structure enables him to run all day in the field if he has to, or to look like he's floating around a show ring.

Two Sizes Fit All

The AKC breed standard divides Beagles into two varieties based on size: under thirteen inches in height when measured at the withers (the top of the shoulder), and over thirteen but not exceeding fifteen inches in height. In the show ring, these two sizes compete separately. Beagles who are taller than fifteen inches cannot be entered in field trials or shows. In general, though, Beagles tend to vary from about ten to sixteen inches at the withers.

Beagles under thirteen inches should weigh less than twenty pounds. Dogs from thirteen to fifteen inches weigh from twenty to thirty pounds.

According to the standard, there's no height or weight difference between males and females.

Body, Neck, Chest, and Shoulders

The Beagle standard has 100 points, and each feature of the dog is assigned a certain number of those points. The number of points is based on how important those features are to the breed overall. The highest number of points is given to the body (35) and the running gear (30), which includes the forelegs, hips, thighs, hind legs, and feet.

The key to evaluating a Beagle's conformation is assessing the overall picture. Basically, a good Beagle will be square in appearance, have good bone or substance, and have straight front legs. Look for a deep chest with an area that

Beagles were built to run and chase with tenacity and courage.

What's a Pocket Beagle?

Paintings from the days of Queen Elizabeth I (1533–1603) depict short-legged, somewhat pointy-nosed Beagles measuring nine inches at the withers. These were referred to as Pocket Beagles. Even shorter dogs, called Glove Beagles, were small enough to be held in a gauntlet—a glove of armored leather with a long sleeve. These dogs were also popular with the royal family.

Today there are very few *really* small Beagles of the size shown in those paintings. If a breeder tells you that she has one, it's not because the dog is just little, but rather because the Beagle suffers from dwarfing or chondrodystrophy, a serious physical deformity and an inherited health disorder.

Even if the parents of a puppy are under thirteen inches, breeders do not have a crystal ball to predict what size a puppy will grow up to be. If a breeder tells you differently, they're mistaken. If you want a Beagle under thirteen inches, wait until the dog is nine months old and full grown, and you'll know for sure.

curves upward behind the ribs and before the pelvis (this is known as the *tuck-up*). His hindquarters are strong and well-angulated. This refers to the angles that are formed by the bones of the hip, pelvis, thigh, and feet.

There should be symmetry and fluidity in his motion. Proportion and balance are important dimensions in assessing good Beagle type.

It is understandable why the authors of the standard would put so much emphasis on the body and the running gear. Originally, these dogs were expected to hunt for hours over all types of terrain and, through courage, patience, and persistence, overtake a hare capable of reaching speeds of forty miles per hour.

Unable to run that fast themselves, the little hounds had to use their highly developed sense of smell, pack instincts, and intelligence to stay in the chase until their quarry was tired. Therefore, all the emphasis is on strength; propelling power; sound, firm feet; freedom of action; ample lung capacity; and other structural traits.

Of course, having a white tip on the end of the tail makes it easier for the hunter to keep a Beagle in sight when the dog is far out in front.

Head

Why is the head given so many points (25)? When the cranium is described as "full and broad," this assumes the dog is very brainy. The wide nostrils and the moderately long, straight muzzle should help with the olfactory wizardry required of a hound who is expected to follow the trail of the rabbit—the game animal that leaves the least amount of scent of any quarry.

Eyes

Soft and houndlike, gentle and pleading, those brown or hazel eyes are a window into the Beagle's good nature. The typical Beagle expression is just one of the things that make him so compelling. Looking into a Beagle's eyes should reveal the honesty, loyalty, affection, and intelligence that make the Beagle so beloved in the field, in the home, and in the show ring.

The eyes should be brown or hazel, large, and set well apart. They should give the Beagle a gentle and pleading expression. Those soft eyes are also responsible for all the treats people just can't resist handing out.

Sweet, round eyes and long, low-set ears characterize the Beagle's head.

Ears

A pretty head usually has pretty ears to go with it. Beagle ears are very distinctive. Sitting low on the head, they're long and should reach almost to the end of the dog's nose. Turning slightly toward the cheek, the ear is rounded at the tip and should never stand up.

Beagles have long ears so that they can pick up scent from the ground. Besides, who can resist stroking that soft face and fingering those luxurious flaps? Just keep them out of the water bowl. When Beagles drink water, those ears have a way of going for a swim.

Because of the length of ear flap covering the ear canal, Beagles do tend to get ear infections. Keep the ears clean and dry and your dog shouldn't have any problems.

Coat and Colors

The Beagle has a medium-length double coat. This means that his outercoat is hard and protects the dog from brush and bad weather. The outercoat should lie smooth against the body. Underneath that topcoat is a finer undercoat.

Although most people think that all Beagles are the traditional tri-color pattern of black, brown, and white, according to the standard, any hound color is acceptable. What's a hound color? Hound colors include all shades and combinations of white or cream, black, tan/lemon/red, brown/liver, and blue/gray, and the colors of the hare or badger.

The second most popular color combination is red and white, sometimes described as lemon and white or tan and white. Tri-color patterns can also be faded or diluted colors such as blue, deep brown (chocolate), liver, or lilac. Two large patches of two or more colors on the Beagle's sides or across the back are referred to as *piebald*. Badger-pied is a pale cream with blended black, silver, and fawn, which resembles a badger's coat.

Another color, Belvoir tan, is named after the famous Belvoir pack in Britain. The Belvoir hounds had a distinctive tan coloration that was all the rage in the 1890s. If a hound has flecks of color, either tan (red) or muted black (blue), this pattern is called *ticking*. When someone refers to a blueticked Beagle, the name refers to the coloration.

A mottled coat has round, dark blotches on top of a lighter coat color.

Temperament

Happy-go-lucky—this accurately describes the Snoopy dog everyone knows and loves. If a shy Beagle does come along, it usually means he wasn't properly socialized when he was a puppy or that his ancestors were shy.

Unless they're having a food fight, aggressive Beagles are rare.

Beagles should be sweet and family-oriented.

Chapter 2

Beagle History

Tracking down the Beagle's ancestors takes more than a pack of hounds. One of the oldest breeds in history, no one really knows the exact time and place when the first Beagle appeared.

What little we do know about the breed comes from the Greek historian Xenophon, who wrote about small hounds that pursued hare and rabbit in ancient Greece. These dogs were used to hunt for food rather than for sport, so little consideration was given to the way the dogs looked or their style of hunting. Basically, the dogs helped locate the hare in open fields by scent and drove it into long nets for capture. Traders first brought these dogs to Europe. By the fourteenth century, they could be found in Britain, where small game was abundant and hunting was avidly pursued.

Hounds in England

The hounds' scenting ability was legendary, and once the British hunters learned of their prowess, the dogs were welcome acquisitions. According to the *Oxford English Dictionary*, the word *beagle* first appeared in the English language in 1475.

By the sixteenth century, Queen Elizabeth I (1533–1603) had a pack of little hounds called Beagles, as did most noblemen. These dogs had short legs and pointed faces, and did not look like the Beagles we know today. They measured barely nine inches at the withers and many were small enough to be carried in baskets on horseback on the way to hunts. These dogs were known as Pocket or Glove Beagles because they fit in the horsemen's pockets or could be held in a gauntlet (a glove of armored leather with a long sleeve). The small hounds would slowly and methodically search out their quarry, which ran in intricate patterns to confuse their pursuers.

By the beginning of the eighteenth century, many upper-class men, who had time for such things, appreciated the pleasure of hunting with a pack of well-bred Beagles. But by the middle of the same century, a new generation of hunters wanted a more exciting and quicker-paced chase with faster hounds. The fox-hunt became all the rage.

Foxhounds were developed by crossing the Buck Hound (a larger dog already used for hunting fox) and the Beagle. As foxhunting grew in popularity, the Beagle's popularity declined. However, Foxhound packs were larger than Beagle packs, and not every hunter could afford to keep so many dogs. In addition, farmers needed Beagles to clear their land of small game who ruined the crops and to hunt hare and rabbit as a source of food.

Each pack owner bred dogs according to the type of dog he needed. Eventually, two distinct types of hounds developed: the Southern Hound, who

> **Taking Names**
>
> No one knows for sure the actual origin of the name *Beagle*. Possibly, it's derived from the old French *be'geule*, meaning "gape throat" or "open mouth." This might refer to the Beagle's habit of baying or howling when going after quarry. Another possibility is the Old English *begele*, or the French *beigh*, or the Celtic *beag*. All of these words mean "small."

Beagling was very popular by the mid-1800s. Those hunting dogs are the ancestors of the Beagles we see today.

had a compact body, a deep voice, and long ears to trap scent, and was slow and thoughtful; and the North Country Beagle, who was faster and longer-bodied.

Beagling (hunting with Beagles) became more popular in the mid-nineteenth century. The Reverend Phillip Honeywood of Essex developed a pack of Beagles that were excellent hunters. These dogs are the progenitors of the Beagles we see today.

Eventually, people who raised dogs for sport rather than for work became more interested in breeding dogs for specific characteristics and showing off the efforts of their labors at dog shows. The first known dog show was held in Newcastle in 1859 and the Kennel Club was formed in 1873. The Beagle was one of the first recognized breeds. The Beagle Club was formed a few years later, in 1890, with the purpose of standardizing the breed and making it more uniform in looks and temperament. In 1897, the Beagle Club sponsored its first show.

The Beagle in America

Brought to America by the British to help settle the new frontier, the Beagle maintained a rather low profile until the mid-nineteenth century. Actually, a popular favorite of the colonists was the Black-and-Tan Hound, a close relative of the modern Kerry Beagle of Ireland—which is not a Beagle at all, but more of

Beagles were brought to America to hunt. Many still do.

What Is the AKC?

The American Kennel Club (AKC) is the oldest and largest pure-bred dog registry in the United States. Its main function is to record the pedigrees of dogs of the breeds it recognizes. While AKC registration papers are a guarantee that a dog is pure-bred, they are absolutely not a guarantee of the quality of the dog—as the AKC itself will tell you.

The AKC makes the rules for all the canine sporting events it sanctions and approves judges for those events. It is also involved in various public education programs and legislative efforts regarding dog ownership. The AKC has also helped establish a foundation to study canine health issues and a program to register microchip numbers for companion animal owners. The AKC has no individual members—its members are national and local breed clubs and clubs dedicated to various competitive sports.

a multipurpose hound. The Kerry Beagle was Foxhound size and capable of hunting small and large game, day or night. With her short legs, the Beagle resembled a Dachshund or a Basset Hound more than a modern Beagle. But because the hound helped put meat on the table, the dog was highly valued.

The Beagle took on a distinctive look when Norman Elmore and General Richard Rowett, who had a passion for breeding horses and bred the fifteenth winner of the Kentucky Derby, imported foundation Beagle stock from the best working hunting packs in Britain. These dogs were the ancestors of modern Beagles in America. Other huntsmen imported high-quality British Beagles as well. In 1880, Mr. Arnold brought over a pack from the Royal Rock Beagle kennel in the north of England, and James Kernochan imported a Beagle pack in 1896.

To exhibit these dogs in conformation shows, Beagle enthusiasts in Philadelphia organized the first Beagle breed club, the American-English Beagle Club, in 1884. The same year, the American Kennel Club was formed, and a year later it registered its first Beagle, a dog named Blunder.

Forming a Beagle Club

With so much interest in the breed's looks and hunting ability, the National Beagle Club (NBC) was formed in 1888. It merged with the American-English Beagle Club at the end of the nineteenth century. To test the breed's field aptitude, the organization sponsored an informal field trial in 1890. One year later, the club held the first National Beagle Club specialty show (a dog show for just one breed). To put more emphasis on the breed's running ability, the Beagle standard was revised in 1900.

This Beagle is competing in a national field trial. The National Beagle Club promotes the versatile Beagle who can hunt and show like a champ.

To further the club's goals, five members of the NBC purchased land in 1916 to hold regular field trials. Today, the club has access to the 508 acres in Western Loudoun County, Virginia, known as the Institute Farm. It holds field trials for Beagles and Basset Hounds on the property.

Local Beagle clubs under the sponsorship of the NBC soon formed throughout the United States, and these clubs held both field trials and conformation shows. Today there are pack trials, field trials, and the annual Triple Challenge trial, which recognizes and promotes the versatile Beagle in field and conformation events during a weekend of competition. The first Triple Challenge event was held in 1996.

Dual Champions

When a Beagle earns both conformation and field titles, she is awarded the title of Dual Champion. It signifies that the dog is not only good looking, but also possesses the instincts, intelligence, and stamina to run after a rabbit with a

Beagle Events

Brace trial: Two or three Beagles compete and are judged on how well they can trail a rabbit

Bench show: A conformation show where dogs remain on display for spectators to view throughout the day of the show

Conformation show: A judge evaluates each dog on how closely she meets the AKC breed standard

Pack trials: Large packs of thirty or more Beagles hunt hare

Three-hour stakes class: Evaluates the Beagle's field ability and ability to cooperate with packmates; top-placing dogs may be required to run for three hours

Field trials: Tests the individual Beagle's ability to hunt rabbit or hare

Triple challenge trial: A combination of conformation, field trial, and pack hunt

pack. The first Beagle to become a Dual Champion was the fifteen-inch white, black, and tan Ch. Frank Forest (1886–1889). As with many outstanding dogs, he became a major influence in the breed, and many Beagles today have Frank in their pedigrees.

There were many dual champions during the 1940s, then none for about fifty years. Dual Ch. Pebble Ridge Shadrack earned the distinction in the late 1990s.

The Busy Beagle

The pet Beagle today is a product of both field-bred and show-bred Beagles. This versatile breed is an action-packed hound in a small package. She performs well in all dog sports, such as obedience, agility, tracking, and flyball, and enjoys having something to do.

Beagles are pack dogs and need to be part of a group. They'll get along well with other Beagles, but they won't do well left alone all day.

As pack dogs, Beagles have a strong need to be part of a group. When they're left alone for long periods of time, they'll look for anything to do, even if that means digging, barking, and howling. Once she matures at 18 months of age, taking your dog for a long walk or a jog on a leash is a very good idea because it keeps her mind and body occupied.

While the Beagle's inner drive to find a scent may be troublesome in your yard, it's worth its weight in gold in the work force. In a scented world, the Beagle can sniff out things far more efficiently than we ever could. Because of their small size, good disposition, and outstanding sense of smell, Beagles are used by the United States Department of Agriculture at international airports to sniff out illegally imported foodstuffs and plants. Beagles who do this work are part of the USDA's Beagle Brigade. The cheerful little Beagle goes about her job without frightening the travelers and can fit into some tight spots a larger animal could not squeeze into.

Chapter 3

Why Choose a Beagle?

If you watched the 2008 Westminster Kennel Club Dog Show on television, chances are you saw the fifteen-inch tri-color Beagle, Ch. K-Run's Park Me in First, (known as Uno) win Best in Show. The first Beagle in the show's 131-year history to win this prestigious honor, Uno captivated the crowd with his signature *ah-roo* howl and happy-go-lucky attitude. A super dog by any standard, Uno is the epitome of what a Beagle is all about.

Once you've seen Uno—and oh yes, that other Beagle who is also America's favorite hound, Snoopy—it's easy to see why you would want a Beagle. But wait. There are many other reasons why you should (or should not) acquire a little Beagle of your own.

While it's one thing to admire a dog on television or in the comics, it's quite another to actually own one and take care of him for the rest of his life. Whenever a dog becomes a big movie, television, or dog show star, it always spikes an interest in the breed. People rush out and get one because they expect the dog will look and act the same in their own home. But they soon discover that having a dog is just like having a child who needs constant care. Sadly, there are way too many Beagles abandoned each year because the owners decided the breed wasn't right for them.

Even if Beaglemania strikes you, I hope you'll take the time to find out if this breed is really the right lifelong dog for you before you acquire one. Wouldn't you just hate to see a dog like Uno in a shelter?

What's Regal About a Beagle?

A Beagle experiences the world in two ways: through his nose and through his stomach. He dearly loves to hunt, and he is strongly bonded to his packmates, human or canine. Everything else in life is pretty much ho-hum. The Beagle is an easygoing, mellow kind of guy.

If you're unsure about these traits or others, contact a local Beagle club and talk to other Beagle owners. Ask them to tell you about their dogs and what it's like to live with one. Spend time visiting Beagle breeders to learn what they like and don't like about the hound.

Born to Run . . . or Nap

While Beagles today don't have to have extensive periods of exercise every day, they do need to get up and move around from time to time. Beagles were bred to tolerate extended periods of down time in between periods of intense, hard-running exercise.

A healthy dog is an active one, so letting your Beagle lounge on your couch all day is not good for him.

The kennelmen who took care of hunting packs in the old days would run the dogs once or even twice a day. Later kennels in a much faster-paced time were lucky to be able to take the hounds out once or twice a week. So it's possible that a Beagle living in an apartment in the city may get as much exercise as his counterpart living in the country, especially if you like to walk or jog.

A healthy Beagle is an active dog. Yours will need plenty of exercise.

The Dog's Senses

The dog's eyes are designed so that he can see well in relative darkness, has excellent peripheral vision, and is very good at tracking moving objects—all skills that are important to a carnivore. Dogs also have good depth perception. Those advantages come at a price, though: Dogs are nearsighted and are slow to change the focus of their vision. It's a myth that dogs are color-blind. However, while they can see some (but not all) colors, their eyes were designed to most clearly perceive subtle shades of gray—an advantage when they are hunting in low light.

Dogs have about six times fewer taste buds on their tongue than humans do. They can taste sweet, sour, bitter, and salty flavors, but with so few taste buds it's likely that their sense of taste is not very refined.

A dog's ears can swivel independently, like radar dishes, to pick up sounds and pinpoint their location. Dogs can locate a sound in $6/100$ of a second and hear sound four times farther away than we can (which is why there is no reason to yell at your dog). They can also hear sounds at far higher pitches than we can.

In their first few days of life, puppies primarily use their sense of touch to navigate their world. Whiskers on the face, above the eyes, and below the jaws are sensitive enough to detect changes in airflow. Dogs also have touch-sensitive nerve endings all over their bodies, including on their paws.

Smell may be a dog's most remarkable sense. Dogs have about 220 million scent receptors in their nose, compared to about 5 million in humans, and a large part of the canine brain is devoted to interpreting scent. Not only can dogs smell scents that are very faint, but they can also accurately distinguish between those scents. In other words, when you smell a pot of spaghetti sauce cooking, your dog probably smells tomatoes and onions and garlic and oregano and whatever else is in the pot.

Your Beagle doesn't need a large house and yard to be healthy, but going for a long walk every day prevents boredom and keeps his mind active. Whatever exercise you choose should be suited to his age and overall condition.

Beagle Brainiac

When a Beagle wants something he smells, nothing is going to get in his way. The breed is super smart. He understands what his senses are for and uses everything he has to solve problems. Once he finds something, he'll remember where it was forever.

Unfortunately, he has selective hearing as well. The Beagle is a typical hound in that he will go his own way and do things in his own good time. You have to find a way to motivate him to do what you want him to do. You can call him over to you all you want, but if he'd rather do something else, like eat or follow a scent trail, forget about it!

Good with Children

Most Beagles and children are fast friends. There's something magical between them when both kids and dogs respect each other. They can whisper sweet nothings, play hide-and-seek, and fall asleep together on the couch. When the relationship is good, it will stand the test of time. Your child will always remember the Beagle she grew up with.

But children have to be taught how to treat your Beagle. You have to lay down the rules, encourage safe play, and always supervise. A little hound is no babysitter, and a child should never be expected to take care of a dog.

Teach your child not to bother your Beagle while he's eating, playing with a toy, or searching for a scent. And don't let your child jump on your dog, because that can really hurt!

Remember, too, that you're in charge of the doors and gates in your home, and instruct your child never to open them without your permission. It takes only a second for your dog to scoot out the door in search of a particularly delicious aroma.

A Beagle's ears and tail are not for pulling, either. If you want your dog and child to grow up together happily, teach them how to treasure each other.

Hunting Companion

If you live in rabbit country and are looking for a dog who knows his way around a rabbit hole, a Beagle is the breed for you. While other hunting hounds may be specialists in the quarry they chase after, they can't hold a candle to the

Children and Beagles are a good mix.

Beagle in the nose department. Most dogs can follow the scent trail of a deer, but the rabbit and hare have the least amount of scent of any game animal.

Although the Beagle has an extraordinarily well-developed sense of smell, he still has to work hard! The scene goes like this: A cottontail rabbit nibbles the clover at the edge of the woods. The Beagle bounds off toward the woods, his tail up and practically vibrating with excitement.

He drifts over to where the cottontail was dining and his whole body begins to wag. His tail is whipping from side to side as he begins to whimper slightly, then breaks out into a Beagle aria. *Ah-roo, ah-roo!* Soon he is trotting along the line of scent left behind by the rabbit and singing his heart out.

While the new owners of a Beagle puppy may find it amusing that the tiny creature cruises around the house with his nose to the ground, this is both a legacy from his pack-hunting ancestors and a rehearsal for future hunting if given the opportunity.

Within days of settling into his new home, a Beagle will have sniffed out and memorized his territory. His rounds each day will tell him whether anyone new has shown up.

Loves to Vocalize

Ah-roo, ah-roo. That's the baying sound Uno makes, usually for no reason other than to say his piece. Even at the big Westminster Kennel Club Dog Show, where dogs never lower themselves to make noise, Uno's sound machine was more of a croon than a bark. And he did it several times.

The Beagle has a very musical voice (in fact, the term used to describe the unique sound of a particular hound in a pack is his *note*), and while he's not yappy, the Beagle can be quite vocal in expressing himself—especially if a stray dog or cat enters his territory.

This characteristic has led many people to praise the Beagle's usefulness as a watchdog. He will alert his owners when strangers are around, but he is not likely to harm the UPS man. Also, since he has been selectively bred for his voice as well as his nose, his alarm or warning bark often sounds like it comes from a much larger dog—a deterrent to would-be intruders.

Beagles get along really well with other Beagles. The breed was developed to live and work in packs.

Plays Well with Others

Beagles were originally bred to get along in a pack, and this personality trait has served the breed well throughout the generations. Hunting Beagles spent their whole lives in a large group and were selected for sociable personalities. They also had to have the desire and ability to hunt without special training or requiring much direction from people. (Pack dogs learn to hunt from the elders of their own species.)

The Beagle is a bold and friendly little hound, not too wary of strangers, but not too overbearing either. No kennelman caring for a large kennel of hounds would tolerate a fighter, so over the years the aggressive characteristics have been eliminated as quickly as they appeared. Most hunting kennels had large lodging rooms with communal sleeping quarters and large exercise yards. There could be twenty or more hounds in each run, generally separated by sex, so a nonaggressive nature was a priority.

Snuggler Extraordinaire

The Beagle's loyalty, courage, and devotion haven't changed over the centuries. His temperament should be very congenial—assuming, of course, he is well treated.

He responds well to a family or other group of people, rather than just one person as a companion. This doesn't mean he won't be loyal to his owner. He absolutely will, especially if his environment has all the right stuff: comfy beds and a never-empty food dish.

What's Not to Like About a Beagle?

Who doesn't love America's favorite hound? After you learn what some of his bad habits are, though, you might not think this is the breed for you.

Digging

To you, the yard may look like a nice collection of trees and flowers. But to a Beagle, whose main goal in life is to sniff everything in sight, the garden is a place of earthly delights. By scratching at the ground, he can unearth a whole host of fragrances: a small rodent that may live deep underneath, some wet soil where his owner left a track, or maybe the place where the child in the household buried an apple. Anything is possible, but your dog won't know until he's dug it up!

Your Beagle doesn't mean to rearrange the yard, but sometimes dirt happens. If a pristine dream landscape is your priority, you might want to dedicate part of the yard just for your dog. Give him his own digging locale that he can work to his heart's content. Make it really exciting for him and bury some dog toys deep down for him to find on his own.

Howling and Nuisance Barking

Beagles bark. That's what they do. They also howl if they get lonely enough or if the mood strikes them. Maybe you can tolerate the noise because the dog lets you know if there's a stranger at the door and scares off would-be intruders.

Nuisance barking is another thing. It's the top reason people give up their Beagles. To prevent this annoying disturbance, give your dog plenty of exercise and attention when you're home. Consider hiring a dog walker or a pet sitter to take him out while you're gone, or asking a neighbor to visit with him.

Try giving him special toys with food treats inside to keep him occupied when you leave the house so he won't disturb the neighbors. Leaving him indoors when you're gone may help keep the volume down, too.

Dogs do like to have company, and if your dog has a canine buddy he may not feel so lonely when you leave. But if you decide to get another Beagle, you may or may not have less howling to contend with. It all depends on the individual dogs. Sometimes a quiet Beagle will learn from the noisier one that it's okay to speak up. Only get a second dog if you genuinely want one, not just because you think it will quiet the first one.

To quote Snoopy, "There's no sense doing a lot of barking if you don't have a lot to say."

Beagles will bark. There is no way to untrain this behavior. They will also howl if they are lonely—or simply in the mood.

Lives to Eat

If you leave food out unattended, your Beagle will find it and eat it.

Chapter 4

Choosing Your Beagle

After giving this a lot of thought, you've decided that a Beagle is going to be your new BFF. Your next decision is where to find a really good one. Your very own Snoopy is a big commitment because she's going to be with you for the next ten to fifteen years, so take your time and choose wisely.

Check out the National Beagle Club of America's web site for a list of reputable breeders, and talk to rescue group coordinators and Beagle owners for their suggestions on how to pick the perfect dog or puppy.

The Beagle is a very popular dog—she's been a top-ten favorite for years—so you shouldn't have any problems tracking down the right one for you. Breed rescue groups and shelters always have adult Beagles who need homes, and reputable breeders produce enough puppies for people on their waiting lists.

So Many Choices

You just have to decide whether you want an adult or a puppy, a male or a female, or a loveable show prospect, a field dog, or a pampered pet. Size may also matter to you, although even breeders can't guarantee that a Beagle is going to grow up to be thirteen or fifteen inches when they're just puppies. Breeders frequently guess, however, and often they are right.

Personality counts, too, so give some thought to whether you want a cool, calm, and collected hound or a fireball full of go-go energy. Dogs are unique individuals, so think about what kind of canine temperament you're comfortable with and what you want to be doing with your dog.

When it comes to Beagles, the girls and the boys are pretty much the same.

Male or Female?

With Beagles, there's very little difference between the sexes. Both love people and are sweet and outgoing. As a pack breed, the males and the females are very comfortable around other dogs and do all of the Beagle things you want yours to do.

They'll happily follow their noses wherever they lead them and howl to their heart's content. Beagle boys and girls may both work hard to take charge of the household or they may be quite content to stand aside and let someone else be the leader. Which way things go is based on individual temperament, not sex. Both sexes need to be neutered.

If this Beagle will be your only dog, you can choose either a male or a female. But if you have another dog at home you'll want to choose one of the opposite sex. This is not because your Beagle won't get along with a dog of the same sex, but because your other dog may not. Dogs of the opposite sex tend to be more companionable with one another because there's less competition between them.

Color Choices

Beagles come in just about every true hound color, and this covers a wide range. While most people prefer the classic black, white, and tan tri-color, you'll find other tri-color combinations, red and whites, dilutes (a diluted or lighter version

Beagles come in many colors and combinations. All are adorable.

of the normal tri-color) and pieds (one color with a darker shade). Most of the time, these colors are apparent by the time the pups are a few weeks old.

Field, Show, or Pet?

If you're looking for a field Beagle who's been bred specifically to hunt rabbits, go to a reputable breeder who specializes in this type of dog. Field dogs are noisier and have more energy than pet or show dogs. The tendency to bark and howl are traits a field breeder works hard to produce. You cannot teach a field-bred Beagle to be quiet, no matter how you raise her.

A show dog comes as close as possible to the breed standard of what the ideal Beagle should look and act like. Go to dog shows and talk to show breeders before buying a Beagle you intend to pursue a show championship title with. You'll have a better idea what the world of show Beagles is all about. Not every Beagle can be a show dog, so learn as much as you can about the sport before making a commitment.

Both field and show Beagles make great companions. But if you opt for a pet Beagle who doesn't have to do much other than be your best friend, you'll have a much easier time finding the right one. By going to a reputable breeder, you can often get a dog who looks almost like a champion but you'll only have to pay a pet price.

Puppy, Adolescent, or Adult?

All Beagles are wonderful, no matter how old they are. But if you don't know whether you want a 9-week-old puppy, a slightly older pup, or a mature adult, think about your lifestyle. Beagles at every age have different needs. Depending upon how much time you spend at home or at work, you may or may not be able to give a particular dog what she needs.

Wonder Pup

Who doesn't ooh and aah when they see a puppy? Everyone always wants to hold a puppy. But when it comes to taking care of one, that's another story. The advantage to getting a puppy is that you can socialize and train your puppy the way you want right from the start. If she grows up with bad habits, it will be because you encouraged them.

The disadvantage is that you'll have to watch her every minute of the day or put her in a safe, enclosed area when you can't supervise. You'll be responsible for housetraining her and teaching her basic manners, such as not jumping up on strangers and how to walk nicely on a leash.

The youngest you can take your new pup home is about 9 weeks of age. By then she's fully weaned and has learned from her littermates how to get along in a pack and knows what household noises and people are all about.

It really is impossible to resist a puppy. But make sure you're ready for all the extra work.

Adolescent

A slightly older dog has the advantage that what you see is what you get. You won't have to guess how tall she'll be because she's fully grown by the time she's 9 months old. More than likely she's already housetrained. But if not, she's young enough to learn.

She may have some bad habits, so you may have some work ahead of you, but your Beagle teenager has a long life ahead of her and you'll be able to grow old together.

Adult

All adult Beagles deserve to have a forever home. You can retrain a dog at any age, so if she does have any bad habits, you can correct them.

Hopefully, your adult Beagle is healthy and has a good temperament. But sometimes Beagles from animal shelters and rescue groups may not be in the peak of health, or they're not as secure in a new environment as you had hoped. That's okay. You can improve your dog's health with a good diet and exercise and give her some confidence when she learns that you won't abandon her.

Where Do You Get a Beagle?

The two best ways to find a Beagle are to adopt one from a shelter or breed rescue group, or buy one from a reputable breeder. Both types of dogs have pros and cons and may have different needs. Every dog requires time, training, and patience.

Think about these options and carefully evaluate them before deciding whether to adopt or to buy a Beagle. To help you make up your mind, talk to as many rescue volunteers and reputable breeders as you can.

Adopting a Beagle

Sometimes bad things happen to good dogs, and their owners give them up. Maybe the dogs were never trained correctly to begin with and they've become destructive or too noisy for the neighborhood. Or perhaps the family lost their home and had to move into an apartment that doesn't permit dogs. Other Beagles become separated from their owners and are found wandering the streets. Regardless of the reason, the bottom line is that a Beagle needs a new place to hang her leash.

If giving a home to a dog who really needs one warms your heart, you'll find both purebred Beagles and Beagle mixes at a shelter. Sometimes, even puppies are available. It's unusual if you don't find a Beagle when you go to look. But if that's the case, there may be a waiting list you can add your name to.

Plenty of good dogs need homes. An adult Beagle can make a great pet.

The Beagle you find may already be spayed or neutered at a shelter. If not, the shelter may reimburse a portion of the veterinary bill once you have it done, and the adoption fee for the dog is less than the purchase price a breeder might charge you.

Unfortunately, most shelters don't have the time, budget, or expertise to match up the right dog with the right owner. Many will not be available to answer any questions you might have after you take your Beagle home. You won't know anything about the dog's background or much about her personality. Some shelter Beagles have behavioral problems that may develop later on, such as separation anxiety or chewing, so you may have to spend more time retraining your dog.

Another way to adopt a Beagle is to contact a breed rescue group. Many have web sites that post photos and descriptions of dogs. The NBC also has information about breed rescue on its web site.

Sadly, there are always more Beagles who need homes than people available to take them in. This is where breed rescue groups become involved. They take in the dogs who would otherwise be killed at a shelter because of overcrowding, and they find foster homes until a permanent owner becomes available.

Rescue groups evaluate the dog to uncover any problems and will provide training if necessary. More than just finding new digs, they're concerned with matching the right owner to the right Beagle so that she becomes a treasured member of the family for the rest of her life.

Buying a Beagle

If you prefer to start out with either a purebred puppy or an adolescent Beagle, your best bet is to buy one from a reputable breeder. Breeders also occasionally have adult dogs available. If they don't have an adult dog, they can probably refer you to another quality breeder who does have one.

Take your time to thoroughly check out the breeder. There are significant differences among breeders—differences that can save you hundreds of dollars in veterinary bills down the road—because not all purebred dogs are created equal. There's more to finding a good Beagle than whether or not a breeder has one available on the day you call and for the price you want to pay.

For the best Beagle puppy or adolescent, contact the NBC for a list of reputable breeders. While you may pay more for a Beagle from someone who shows their dogs than from a breeder who doesn't, you'll get so much more for your money in the long run.

Don't base your decision on which breeder to buy from solely on price. If you cannot afford the purchase price now, you're not going to be able to afford your dog's expenses later on. Veterinary bills, food, grooming, toys, and bedding are more expensive than the dog. Wait and save up your money if you have to so that you can buy a Beagle from a quality breeder.

Reputable breeders have made a lifetime commitment to producing healthy, personable Beagles who are excellent examples of what a beautiful Beagle should look like and act like. They care about the welfare of the breed and usually belong to at least one Beagle club—the NBC and/or a regional club. Connecting with other dedicated breeders provides a network of experienced people who may also have pups or adult dogs available.

Reputable breeders plan litters years in advance and spend a lot of time researching pedigrees before choosing the sire and dam. They spare no expense in providing expert veterinary care for every dog they have. Reputable breeders use the best dogs they possibly can and test them before breeding to make sure they are free from certain genetic illnesses, such as heart problems and hip and elbow dysplasia.

Every sire and dam is AKC-registered. This guarantees that the pedigree, the Beagle's family tree, is accurate. Often the breeder knows the temperament and appearance of every dog on the pedigree going back four or five generations.

When you contact a reputable breeder, expect to be interviewed. The breeder will want to make sure you can provide the right care and training for the Beagle they have worked so hard to produce. The breeder will ask you questions about why you want a Beagle, what you plan to do with your dog, and where you plan to keep her. If they feel you can't give the puppy the right home, they won't sell you a Beagle.

While the breeder is interviewing you, you should also evaluate them. Look at the conditions the pups are raised in. Puppies should be kept indoors so they can interact with people and become accustomed to normal household sounds. If puppies spend their first eight weeks away from a family in outdoor kennels or cages, they tend to be aloof or shy with people later in life.

The puppy area should be clean, well lit, and large enough for the pups to run around freely so they can exercise their little bodies. The mother should look healthy and be friendly and outgoing. If she growls at you, it isn't a good sign. Puppies learn from their mothers, and they will grow up being like their mother.

Why does all of this matter if you only want a pet and not a show dog? Not all of the pups in the litter are show quality, but they're all raised as show pups. Buying from a litter like this gives you a better chance of having a healthy, well-adjusted, physically and mentally sound Beagle.

You're not just buying the puppy, but the breeder's expertise as well. They'll share information with you about Beagle behavior, care, health, and training long after you take the puppy home.

This breeder stands behind the puppies and adolescent dogs they produce and will always care for them. If, at any time and for any reason, you can no longer keep your Beagle, the breeder will take the dog back and try to find a new home for her or keep the dog. No Beagle from a reputable breeder ever winds up unwanted in a shelter.

Reputable breeders make sure all their pups get off to the best possible start.

Picking a Healthy Puppy

Of all the factors you'll consider when you acquire a Beagle, her health is the most important. When you're looking at litters, look for these characteristics.

- The eyes should be clear and without any discharge or redness.
- The puppy should be active and not huddled in a corner or lying down most of the time.
- The coat should be sleek and shiny, not thin, patchy, or dry.
- The puppy should have dry, odor-free ears.
- The puppy should be eager to greet you and want to crawl into your lap. It's okay if she is playing, but she should come over at least once to check you out.
- The puppy should have a healthy appetite.
- The puppy should not have diarrhea or vomit.

Choosing the pup with the temperament that's right for you is a little less precise. You'll see personality types in every litter, ranging from extremely active to very docile. If you're not sure which appeals to you, choose the pup with the middle mood—not too wild and crazy and not so laidback that you wonder if she's okay. Your puppy's attitude will remain pretty much the same for the rest of her life, so make sure you like it early on.

A healthy puppy looks bright and alert and ready to face the world.

Part II
Caring for Your Beagle

Chapter 5

Getting Ready for Your Beagle

It's almost time to add your new Beagle to your household and it's very exciting. Beaglemania has struck and you can hardly wait to bring your new hound home. Charge up the video camera, because you'll want to capture those first magical moments when your dog makes his grand entrance into your life.

Before the big day, though, there are some things you'll need to do around the house to give him the royal welcome he deserves. First, decide where you want him to spend his time, and then make sure it's Beagle-safe. Next, begin stocking up on the right supplies before his arrival so you can enjoy your new dog without having to run out to the store at the last minute.

Home Makeover: Beagle Edition

It's always amazing how much mischief one little Beagle can stir up—all quite innocently. Getting into trouble is one thing, but hurting himself is another. Your four-footed hound doesn't understand that chewing something that isn't meant for him may cause a life-threatening intestinal blockage, poison him, or electrocute him—to say nothing of incurring your wrath.

Surely you don't want anything to happen to your dog in your home or yard. To make sure your environment is trouble-free, carefully examine every nook and cranny both indoors and out for anything that looks dangerous.

You may want to pack up your most prized possessions or put them out of paw's reach until your pup is done with the chew-up-everything-in-sight stage.

This could last a year or two, depending on your Beagle buddy. If this seems a little drastic, just think of how you're going to feel if you come home and see an irreplaceable family heirloom dangling from your Beagle's teeth.

Another option to safeguard your collectibles is to close the doors or use baby gates to block off the rooms you don't want your dog wandering through. These temporary gates will also come in handy if you need to keep your dog confined for a short time, for example if you have repair people working in your home or you want to block off the staircase.

Indoor Hangouts

Before you bring your Beagle home, decide what rooms in the house he will spend most of his time in. He should sleep indoors with the family, preferably in a crate, so you'll need to choose a location for the crate that's not too warm or too drafty for your dog.

While the Sealy mattress company says that 67 percent of pet owners let their pets sleep in their bed, that's not a good place for a new dog. He needs to know he has a safe spot of his own for snoozing, and so do you. He should sleep in his crate, but put the crate in the same room you sleep in. Beagles like to stay with their pack—and you are his pack—so this is ideal. Your dog can be with you and

Little bitty puppies can get into great big trouble. Limit where your dog is allowed in the house when he's still young.

Puppy-Proofing Your Home

You can prevent much of the destruction puppies can cause and keep your new dog safe by looking at your home and yard from a dog's point of view. Get down on all fours and look around. Do you see loose electrical wires, cords dangling from the blinds, or chewable shoes on the floor? Your pup will see them, too!

In the kitchen:

- Put all knives and other utensils away in drawers.
- Get a trash can with a tight-fitting lid.
- Put all household cleaners in cupboards that close securely; consider using childproof latches on the cabinet doors.

In the bathroom:

- Keep all household cleaners, medicines, vitamins, shampoos, bath products, perfumes, makeup, nail polish remover, and other personal products in cupboards that close securely; consider using childproof latches on the cabinet doors.
- Get a trash can with a tight-fitting lid.
- Don't use toilet bowl cleaners that release chemicals into the bowl every time you flush.
- Keep the toilet bowl lid down.
- Throw away potpourri and any solid air fresheners.

In the bedroom:

- Securely put away all potentially dangerous items, including medicines and medicine containers, vitamins and supplements, perfumes, and makeup.
- Put all your jewelry, barrettes, and hairpins in secure boxes.
- Pick up all socks, shoes, and other chewables.

inhale your scent all night long and not feel abandoned. The last thing you want in the middle of the night is to hear your Beagle howling in an effort to locate you.

Once you figure out the sleeping arrangements, pick a dining spot. Feeding your dog and giving him water in the kitchen is probably the easiest. You won't

In the rest of the house:

- Tape up or cover electrical cords; consider childproof covers for unused outlets.
- Knot or tie up any dangling cords from curtains, blinds, and the telephone.
- Securely put away all potentially dangerous items, including medicines and medicine containers, vitamins and supplements, cigarettes, cigars, pipes and pipe tobacco, pens, pencils, felt-tip markers, craft and sewing supplies, and laundry products.
- Put all houseplants out of reach.
- Move breakable items off low tables and shelves.
- Pick up all chewable items, including television and electronics remote controls, cell phones, MP3 players, shoes, socks, slippers and sandals, food, dishes, cups and utensils, toys, books and magazines, and anything else that can be chewed on.

In the garage:

- Store all gardening supplies and pool chemicals out of reach of the dog.
- Store all antifreeze, oil, and other car fluids securely, and clean up any spills by hosing them down for at least ten minutes.
- Put all dangerous substances on high shelves or in cupboards that close securely; consider using childproof latches on the cabinet doors.
- Pick up and put away all tools.
- Sweep the floor for nails and other small, sharp items.

In the yard:

- Put the gardening tools away after each use.
- Make sure the kids put away their toys when they're finished playing.
- Keep the pool covered or otherwise restrict your pup's access to it when you're not there to supervise.
- Secure the cords on backyard lights and other appliances.
- Inspect your fence thoroughly. If there are any gaps or holes in the fence, fix them.
- Make sure you have no toxic plants in the garden.

have to worry about water dribbling on the carpet, and your dog can chow down his meals at the same time that you eat yours.

When he's not eating or sleeping, it's a good idea to set up some dog-free zones around the house, such as the dining and living rooms or your home office. These are places you absolutely don't want your dog to go at any time.

Perhaps you're worried about the new carpet in those rooms or there are too many knick-knacks lying around that he might find tasty. At least until he's thoroughly housetrained and you know that he won't be destructive, he doesn't need the whole house to run amok in.

Before your Beagle comes home, make sure that everything is Beagle-proof. Follow the suggestions in the box on page 46, and he's going to be very safe at home.

Outdoor Safety Zones

Your Beagle will appreciate having enough room in the yard to run around in. But regardless of what size your yard is, it definitely needs to be securely fenced and have gates with strong locks that won't open accidentally. If a Beagle wants something he gets a whiff of on the other side of the fence, he'll think nothing of slipping out the gate if it's left open for even a second. Make it a point to inspect the fence and gates regularly for any holes or gaps that your escape artist might find before you do.

What about getting an electric invisible fence? This may seem like a great idea, especially if you want to keep your dog on your own property and still preserve your view. But you can't rely on it to contain your dog. The way these fences work, underground wiring is installed around the perimeter of your yard and your dog wears a special collar. If he approaches the perimeter, the collar gives him a mild electric shock.

You would think the shock would teach your dog not to go near the fence line again, but that doesn't always happen. Many Beagles don't care about the shock because the lure of what's beyond the fence is much stronger. Once out of the yard, if your dog tries to come back in, he receives another shock. Even if he wants to come home, the thought of receiving another shock may stop him.

Another disadvantage to this system is that it doesn't prevent other dogs, animals, or people from coming into the yard. Unless he's willing to be shocked again, your dog can't get away from intruders.

Outdoors, your dog must always have access to fresh, clean water.

Now that the fence issue is settled, do a clean sweep of your yard to check what plants are growing there. Many are poisonous if your dog decides to snack on them.

Your dog will need a shady location in a corner of your yard where he can cool off on a hot summer's day. A patio cover, shade cloth, or trees will do the trick. He'll also need access to clean, fresh water every moment that he's outdoors.

> **TIP**
>
> For a list of poisonous plants, including photographs of them, check out the web site of the Department of Animal Science at Cornell University, www.ansci.cornell.edu/plants.

Beagle Stuff

Other than worrying about maxing out their credit cards, people love to buy stuff for their dogs. The American Pet Products Manufacturers Association estimates that pet owners in the United States spent $43.4 billion on pet supplies and medicine in 2008. This figure has more than doubled since 1994, so this trend is not going to end any time soon.

The box on page 50 gives you a list of things you will need to get *before* your dog comes home. Choose wisely. Price and quality vary greatly from place to place, so shop around and compare.

Think about size and appropriateness when you're buying toys for your Beagle.

Puppy Essentials

You'll need to go shopping *before* you bring your puppy home. There are many, many adorable and tempting items at pet supply stores, but these are the basics.

- **Food and water dishes.** Look for bowls that are wide and low or weighted in the bottom so they will be harder to tip over. Stainless steel bowls are a good choice because they are easy to clean (plastic never gets completely clean) and almost impossible to break. Avoid bowls that place the food and water side by side in one unit—it's too easy for your dog to get his water dirty that way.
- **Leash.** A six-foot leather leash will be easy on your hands and very strong.
- **Collar.** Start with a nylon buckle collar. For a perfect fit, you should be able to insert two fingers between the collar and your pup's neck. Your dog will need larger collars as he grows up.
- **Crate.** Choose a sturdy crate that is easy to clean and large enough for your puppy to stand up, turn around, and lie down in.
- **Nail cutters.** Get a good, sharp pair that are the appropriate size for the nails you will be cutting. Your dog's breeder or veterinarian can give you some guidance here.
- **Grooming tools.** Different kinds of dogs need different kinds of grooming tools. See chapter 7 for advice on what to buy.
- **Chew toys.** Dogs *must* chew, especially puppies. Make sure you get things that won't break or crumble off in little bits, which the dog can choke on. Very hard plastic bones are a good choice. Dogs love rawhide bones, too, but pieces of the rawhide can get caught in your dog's throat, so they should only be allowed when you are there to supervise.
- **Toys.** Watch for sharp edges and unsafe items such as plastic eyes that can be swallowed. Many toys come with squeakers, which dogs can also tear out and swallow. All dogs will eventually destroy their toys; as each toy is torn apart, replace it with a new one.

A New Leash on Life

Don't even think of taking your Beagle out without a leash. This is a scenthound, and his nose will take him wherever he wants to go. Even field Beagles are taken to the field on a leash and aren't let off until they begin the hunt.

Your dog's leash needs to be sturdy enough that it won't break. Leather is the strongest and will last forever—if your dog doesn't use it as a chew toy. Choose a width that fits comfortably in your hand.

Do not buy a retractable leash. While this may look like a fun way to give your dog more room to roam, it can also be deadly. In fact, these leashes are banned on dog show grounds. If your dog is at the end of the ten-foot length and a menacing loose dog suddenly approaches, you won't be able to reel yours in quickly enough to protect him.

Collar and I.D., Please

This is one doggy item where size really matters. You want a collar to fit snugly when your Beagle is wearing it, so don't get one that's too big now, thinking that he'll grow into it. You don't want it slipping completely off his head. Be a big spender and plan on buying a few different collars as your dog grows.

There are three ways to help the person who finds your Beagle locate you: putting an identification tag on your dog's collar; microchipping him so someone can take him to the veterinarian or local shelter to use their scanner to read his microchip; or putting a global positioning system (GPS) on his collar so you can locate your dog yourself by turning on your computer or cell phone.

A tag should have your name, address, and phone number clearly printed on it, and it should be firmly attached to your dog's collar at all times. Use an O ring (rather than an S hook) to attach the tag to your dog's collar. S hooks are

A good-quality leather leash is easy on your hands and will last for many years.

TIP

Keep current identification on your dog's collar at all times. This helps reunite you with him if he ever becomes lost or stolen. Despite your best intentions, dogs do disappear. More than 5 million pets are reported missing every year.

TIP

If your address or phone number changes, be sure to change your dog's identification tag and notify your veterinarian and the company where you registered your dog's microchip. Whoever finds your dog needs to be able to locate you immediately.

difficult to open and close and for a puppy who is low to the ground, S hooks can catch on things and cause your dog to choke.

Having your dog microchipped at the veterinarian's office is a permanent way to identify him. Only veterinarians and shelters have microchip scanners that can read the information about who owns the dog. A microchip is about the size of a grain of rice and your veterinarian inserts it between your dog's shoulder blades. Don't worry, your dog won't feel a thing.

After the procedure, you'll receive a special tag containing the microchip information, which you can add to your dog's collar. Be sure to send in the paperwork containing your dog's

ID tags will ensure that your dog always comes back to you.

microchip number and your contact information. This registers the microchip and adds it to the recovery system.

The newest way to find your dog if he becomes separated from you is through a GPS device. This high-tech locator is expensive—about $300—but it's fool-proof as long as the special collar containing the GPS isn't removed or falls off your dog. The GPS is small and sturdy and weighs less than three ounces. It connects via satellite to software on your cell phone or computer. Waterproof and noninvasive to your dog, it works indoors as well as out and can even track your dog in heavily wooded areas.

A Crate Is Great

A crate may seem like a dog jail if you've never used one before, but it's actually one of the most useful things you can have for your dog. Think of it as a safe, cozy spot for your Beagle to enjoy some down time, away from the hustle and bustle of a busy household. It's also a must for housetraining, sleeping, hotel stays, and airline travel.

You really only need one crate in the house. If you can afford a second crate and your car has room for a crate, consider buying a second one to keep in the car. A crate in the car is the safest place for him because it provides protection in case of an accident.

A crate will become your dog's home away from home. Show dogs love to nestle into theirs because they are familiar and private.

No room for a crate in the car? Think about buying a doggy booster seat instead. This dog-safe perch buckles into the car seat belt and has a safety harness. Your Beagle will love it because he can see out the window.

You'll find many types of crates to choose from, including hard-sided, soft-sided collapsible, and fold-down wire. To decide which one to buy, think about how your dog will be using it. If you plan on air travel with your dog, airlines require Beagle-size dogs to ride in a hard-sided, airline-approved model. A soft-sided collapsible crate comes in very handy if you're going to be driving with your dog and staying in a hotel.

If you're more of a homebody, you can use any style crate in the house. Wire is great during warm weather because the air circulates, and your Beagle can stay cool and comfortable. When the temperature drops, you can put a fitted cover around the wire crate or use a hard-sided crate, which stays toasty inside.

Be sure to add some comfy bedding inside the crate. Hold off buying expensive cushions until you know if your dog is a cushion chewer. For the first few weeks, use old blankets that are easy to wash. Add dog toys and a soft stuffed animal he can cuddle up against.

Cleanup Supplies

Don't forget about buying cleanup supplies. You'll find enzymatic cleaners at most pet supply stores and online. The enzymes in pet cleaners get rid of elimination odors that only your dog can detect. If he can't smell them, he won't be tempted to return and urinate or defecate there again.

Taking your dog outdoors for a walk or an outing in the car? Don't leave home without bringing something along to pick up your dog's waste. You can keep a small shovel and a stack of bags in your car so you won't forget.

Bringing Beagleman Home

You've prepared the house, bought the supplies, and your dog is at least 9 weeks of age. Now the big day is here and you're ready to pick up The Beagleman.

Your dog may not share your enthusiasm and may even be a little nervous on the way home. To avoid carsickness, ask his breeder or the rescue coordinator not to feed your Beagle any breakfast on the day you bring him home. He can easily wait to eat until an hour or two after he's settled into his new digs.

The First Day

Your dog's first day with you should be planned in advance so he has time to adapt to you without feeling rushed. The best time to pick up your dog is on your day off, first thing in the morning, so you have the whole day together.

Hold off introducing him to the extended family and the whole neighborhood until he has had a few days to settle into your schedule and time to bond with you. Hold off on giving him all the toys you've purchased for him because you don't want to give him so many options all at once. Begin establishing a regular schedule for when your dog will eat, go to the bathroom, play, and sleep. This way he'll know what is expected of him and how to behave in his new environment.

Your new dog may feel a little nervous at first. Give him time to adjust to his new home.

Introducing Other Pets

Be sure to introduce your new Beagle to other pets in the home slowly and gradually. Choose an outdoor area that's neutral territory for them to meet for the first time. This way your first dog or cat won't feel threatened by the newcomer and see the need to protect home turf. Don't leave pets alone together in the beginning. You'll need to supervise them until you know for sure they're all getting along.

Beagles are accustomed to getting along with other dogs, so you shouldn't have much of a problem, but it's better to be safe than sorry later on. Beagles do well with cats, but if you have a pet rabbit, keep this furry companion out of your dog's sight. Remember, the Beagle has been bred for generations to find and chase rabbits, not play with them.

Chapter 6

Feeding Your Beagle

I f your dog could sing, her favorite song would be "Food, Glorious Food!" Beagles love, love, love to eat, and they think every meal should be Thanksgiving dinner. Your job is to feed your dog a healthy diet without letting her become overweight.

Since she can't shop and cook for herself, you're in charge of what goes into her bowl. Today there is more information about the best canine nutrition than ever before. Chances are you won't be feeding your Beagle the same way her ancestors were fed.

How Hounds Were Fed

In the days of the larger hunting kennels, feeding the hounds was a separate job. People believed that hounds, like their wolf ancestors, needed a lot of meat to maintain their fitness. Not much consideration was given to the later stages of life, because a hound's longevity was determined by her useful life in the pack.

Also, most kennels were able to farm out their puppies with local supporters of the hunt (usually farmers), a practice known as sending the puppy out "at walk." This meant that in addition to the puppies being socialized by the farmer's family, exposed to livestock that they would be taught not to chase, and protected from diseases as much as possible, they had access to puppy foods such as milk and cooked table scraps.

By the time a puppy returned to the kennel at about 1 year of age, she was ready for grown-up food. In most cases, that consisted of meat mixed with grain porridge. The kennelman would travel to the farms in the hunt's country and pick up sick, aged, or dead livestock; bring it back to the kennel; and prepare it for the hounds. The amount of meat in proportion to the gruel would be adjusted based on the amount of work the hounds were doing.

In summer, when the hounds were not hunting, they would get a much less nutrient-dense feed, with the exception of the brood bitches. When the hounds were hunting, and therefore getting more animal protein, they actually were allowed to adopt a more wolflike eating pattern of gorge-and-rest, usually being fed only three times a week.

In the old days, hunting hounds ate lots of meat when they were hunting.

Commercial Dog Foods

Watch enough television and you'll see a constant stream of dog food commercials. But before you rush out and buy the latest canine recipe you've seen on the flat screen, take a few moments to find out what's inside those bags and cans of dog food. How do you know what your Beagle should eat?

Read the labels and compare ingredients. Look for a food that provides a well-balanced diet containing proteins, carbohydrates, fats, vitamins, and minerals. Avoid foods that use fillers, which tend to produce volume when combined with gastric juices in a dog's stomach. Some fillers are corn and wheat gluten, cellulose (sawdust, really), and beet pulp (the dried residue from sugar beets, which has no nutritional value).

There are three types of commercial dog foods: dry, canned, and semimoist. Each has advantages and disadvantages, but the one selling point for commercial food is that you only have to open the package, pour it into a bowl, and your Beagle can do what she loves to do best—eat!

Dry food, or kibble, consists of baked morsels made from grains, meats, vegetables, fruits, vitamins, and supplements. It's easy to take with you if you're traveling. And because it's crunchy and abrasive, it helps wipe the tartar off the teeth and keeps them cleaner. It's also the least expensive way to feed your dog.

Reading Dog Food Labels

Dog food labels are not always easy to read, but if you know what to look for they can tell you a lot about what your dog is eating.

- The label should have a statement saying the dog food meets or exceeds the American Association of Feed Control Officials (AAFCO) nutritional guidelines. If the dog food doesn't meet AAFCO guidelines, it can't be considered complete and balanced, and can cause nutritional deficiencies.
- The guaranteed analysis lists the minimum percentages of crude protein and crude fat and the maximum percentages of crude fiber and water. AAFCO requires a minimum of 18 percent crude protein for adult dogs and 22 percent crude protein for puppies on a dry matter basis (that means with the water removed; canned foods will have less protein because they have more water). Dog food must also have a minimum of 5 percent crude fat for adults and 8 percent crude fat for puppies.
- The ingredients list the most common item in the food first, and so on until you get to the least common item, which is listed last.
- Look for a dog food that lists an animal protein source first, such as chicken or poultry meal, beef or beef byproducts, and that has other protein sources listed among the top five ingredients. That's because a food that lists chicken, wheat, wheat gluten, corn, and wheat fiber as the first five ingredients has more chicken than wheat, but may not have more chicken than all the grain products put together.
- Other ingredients may include a carbohydrate source, fat, vitamins and minerals, preservatives, fiber, and sometimes other additives purported to be healthy.
- Some brands may add artificial colors, sugar, and fillers—all of which should be avoided.

However, some dogs don't think kibble is tasty enough. And there is so much variation in quality and cost that you really need to know which one is best for your dog. Because grains are the primary source of carbohydrates, there's always the potential for grain-related molds and toxins. Some dogs also develop grain allergies or sensitivities.

Better dry foods are more expensive because they use natural antioxidants, such as vitamin E (called tocopherols) and vitamin C instead of preservatives to prevent spoilage.

While dogs love the enticing aroma and better taste of canned food, it has some disadvantages. Canned food is mostly water (usually 75 percent), costs more than dry food, and needs refrigeration after opening. It also tends to stick to the teeth, which leads to plaque buildup and eventually, tooth decay.

Semimoist food is tasty and comes wrapped in convenient packages, but unfortunately is a poor nutritional choice. It's high in sugar, artificial colors, and additives—none of which your dog needs.

With dog foods, you usually get what you pay for. The more expensive brands really do offer better nutrition.

Puppy, Adult, and Senior Diets

Depending on their ages and activity levels, dogs have different nutritional requirements. When shopping for commercial food, you'll find recipes for puppies, adults, and seniors.

Puppy Food

Your Beagle puppy grows fast, and she needs more calories as she grows. But not just any calories will do. She needs a high-quality, nutrient-dense recipe for proper growth, with higher protein and fat contents than adult dogs require.

Choose a dry food specially formulated for puppies with at least 24 percent protein and 18 percent fat. The first ingredient should be a whole protein source, such as beef, chicken, turkey, lamb, or fish. Your pup does not need extra calcium or other supplements.

> **TIP**
>
> Expect to pay more for healthier foods. You'll get what you pay for, and you'll see improved health and vigor in your Beagle if you spend a little more for higher-quality foods with fresher, whole ingredients and fewer chemicals.

Growing puppies need more calories, protein, and fat than adult dogs need.

A good canned food puppy recipe has about 9 percent protein and 7 percent fat. If you want to use canned food, add a tablespoon of it to the dry food.

How long should you feed your Beagle puppy food? Most breeders recommend 9 months to 1 year old.

Because their tummies are small, puppies need to eat more frequent meals than adult dogs to feel satisfied. At 9 weeks of age, your puppy needs to eat three or four times a day. Sometime around 4 to 5 months of age, eliminate lunch because your pup no longer needs to eat that extra meal. Instead, divide up that amount of food and give it to your pup during the other meals.

By the time your pup is a year old, she should eat two meals a day.

Adult Food

Once dogs are done growing, they require fewer calories than puppies do. But good nutrition should always be a priority. A good adult dry food formula should contain no less than 22 percent protein and 12 percent fat. Quality canned should contain no less than 8 percent protein and 5 percent fat.

For Beagles who hunt and need peak performance, there are new grain-free recipes that contain a much higher percentage of protein, fat, calories, calcium, and phosphorus that provide additional energy.

Senior Food

People once believed that Beagles over the age of 7 required less protein than they did in their younger days. But veterinary researchers have found that isn't the case. Older Beagles in good health with normal results on blood tests can eat the same food as younger adults. However, less protein may be beneficial to dogs with kidney problems. Talk to your veterinarian.

Homemade Diets

Another option is to make your dog's food. This way you can control all the ingredients in her diet. This may be especially important for dogs with health problems or several dogs with different needs. Holistic veterinarians also believe that your dog will be healthier. Plan on spending more money than you would if you bought commercial food.

A good homemade diet does not mean feeding your dog whatever leftovers you have from your own meals. It does mean maintaining a good nutritional balance while offering variety. Include animal proteins, a fat source including essential fatty acids, minerals including calcium and phosphorus, and a supplement containing vitamins and trace elements.

You have to be organized to feed a homemade diet. It helps to have a steady supply of ingredients on hand. To save time, you can prepare your dog's meal at

Healthy snacks and chews are important throughout a dog's life.

Pet Food vs. People Food

Many of the foods we eat are excellent sources of nutrients—after all, we do just fine on them. But dogs, like us, need the right combination of meat and other ingredients for a complete and balanced diet, and a bowl of meat doesn't provide that. In the wild, dogs eat the fur, skin, bones, and guts of their prey, and even the contents of the stomach.

This doesn't mean your dog can't eat what you eat. A little meat, dairy, bread, some fruits, or vegetables as a treat are great. Just remember, we're talking about the same food you eat, not the gristly, greasy leftovers you would normally toss in the trash. Stay away from sugar, too, and remember that chocolate and alcohol are toxic to dogs.

If you want to share your food with your dog, be sure the total amount you give her each day doesn't make up more than 15 percent of her diet, and that the rest of what you feed her is a top-quality complete and balanced dog food. (More people food could upset the balance of nutrients in the commercial food.)

Can your dog eat an entirely homemade diet? Certainly, if you are willing to work at it. Any homemade diet will have to be carefully balanced, with all the right nutrients in just the right amounts. It requires a lot of research to make a proper homemade diet, but it can be done. It's best to work with a veterinary nutritionist.

CAUTION

Never give your dog cooked bones! They may splinter and cause intestinal obstruction or damage.

the same time you fix your own. A homemade diet needs to be refrigerated and stored properly, because it must be fresh.

Many dog owners claim that feeding their dogs a homemade diet cleared up health issues, such as allergies and skin and coat conditions, and even reduced the number of seizures in epileptic dogs. Generally, they say fresh food gave their dogs more vitality.

A Raw Diet

Other dog owners are big fans of the BARF diet. This is an acronym for *bones and raw food.* This recipe is based entirely on feeding your dog raw meats, vegetables, and bones. Holistic veterinarians and a growing number of dog owners claim that raw food helps keep the teeth clean, contributes to a glossier coat, and ends food allergies.

Traditional veterinarians and other dog owners argue that a raw diet causes salmonella and other bacterial poisoning, and that some dogs develop diarrhea and vomiting. While most dogs digest raw bones without a problem, there is always the chance that a raw bone can cause internal injuries or choking.

A raw diet takes time to prepare, but today there are several dog food companies that sell frozen raw food for dogs. These are available online or through small, independent pet supply stores. To decide if you should switch your dog's diet, consult with your veterinarian.

Dangerous Foods

According to the American Society for the Prevention of Cruelty to Animals (ASPCA), there are a few foods and beverages that are toxic to dogs and should never be given to your Beagle:

- **Alcoholic beverages:** Alcohol causes disorientation and vomiting. Even a small amount can cause serious intoxication and be deadly.
- **Avocado:** Avocado contains persin, a toxin that damages the heart and lungs. If a dog swallows the pit, it can become lodged in the intestinal tract and must be surgically removed.
- **Chocolate and coffee (all forms):** Chocolate and coffee contain caffeine and theobromine, a compound that is a cardiac stimulant and a diuretic, which causes vomiting, rapid breathing, seizures, and sometimes death.
- **Fatty foods:** Fatty and fried foods can cause liver damage.
- **Garlic:** Onions and garlic contain the toxic ingredient thiosulphate, a substance that can break down red blood cells, leading to a very serious condition called Heinz body hemolytic anemia. Symptoms may include pale gums, blood in the urine, lethargy, depression, weakness, and rapid heartbeat. The symptoms usually appear a few days after the food has been eaten, when the toxin has destroyed a significant number of the dog's red blood cells.
- **Grapes and raisins:** Grapes and raisins can cause vomiting, diarrhea, abdominal pain, and lethargy.
- **Macadamia nuts:** Macadamia nuts can cause weakness, muscle tremors, or paralysis in the hindquarters.

Never feed your dog cooked bones, which can splinter and cause him harm. Raw bones can be a great treat.

- **Moldy or spoiled foods:** Spoiled food carries disease-causing germs and bacteria.
- **Onions and onion powder:** Onions, like garlic, are toxic in any form: raw, cooked or dehydrated.
- **Excess salt:** In large quantities, salt leads to electrolyte imbalances and kidney problems. Dogs may also drink too much water.
- **Uncooked yeast dough:** Rising yeast dough can lead to rupture of the digestive system.
- **Products sweetened with xylitol:** Xylitol is an artificial sweetener used in diet products. It can cause a sudden drop in blood sugar, resulting in liver damage.

Avoiding Beagle Bulk

Veterinarians estimate that 25 percent of all dogs are obese. With Beagles, who think that dining should be a canine sport, it's always a challenge to keep them at an average weight. Keeping your dog at a trim weight isn't about beauty, it's about maintaining good health. Packing on too many pounds leads to diabetes, orthopedic problems, heart disease, and other health problems in dogs, just as it does in people.

How can you tell if your Beagle is overweight? Stand over her and look at the outline of her body. Does it resemble an hourglass or a sausage? You should see an indentation in her sides three-quarters of the way down her body. Another way to tell is to feel her sides. You should be able to easily feel (but not see) slight, not bony, protrusions, which are her ribs. If you can't, she weighs too much.

Healthy adult Beagles under thirteen inches should weigh less than twenty pounds. Thirteen- to fifteen-inch Beagles should weigh from twenty to thirty pounds. If you think your Beagle is too heavy, it's a good idea to take her to your veterinarian for a checkup. She could have a health problem that your veterinarian can detect or rule out.

After receiving a clean bill of health, your Beagle is ready to go on a diet. You don't have to buy special reducing diets. Simply cut down gradually on the amount of food you give her. If she acts really hungry, add more fruits and vegetables to her food bowl. Apples, steamed carrots, green beans, and broccoli make great low-calorie treats, and add bulk to your Beagle's diet. Limit the number of snacks you give her, too. If you insist on giving her an extra bit, make it a piece of apple or a string bean.

Add a few extra walks each week. If your dog hasn't exercised in a while, start slowly with twenty minutes a few times a week. Increase the time and the frequency as she builds her stamina.

Water, Water Everywhere

Water is just as important for your dog as food is. Your Beagle should have clean, fresh water at all times. Use a deep, stainless steel bowl and wash it out frequently. Holistic veterinarians recommend giving your dog filtered water. Fluoride and chlorine are present in tap water in most water systems and these minerals may not be healthy for dogs (although so far there is no conclusive evidence about this).

Why do dogs like to drink out of the toilet? With tile floors, bathrooms are usually the coolest room in the house and the water in the bowl stays even colder. It also stays fresh because it's flushed so often!

Chapter 7

Grooming Your Beagle

One of the things pet owners like best about Beagles is that they don't need very much sprucing up to keep them looking clean and healthy. Beagles are basically wash-and-wear dogs.

In the old hunting kennels, Beaglers considered running through wet vegetation as an herbal bath and cedar shavings in the hound's sleeping quarters as an odor reducer. Smelly, oily dressings were used to control external parasites and skin disease.

Grooming methods and ideas have come a long way since then. Today, there are new products and procedures that do a much better job of keeping Beagles fresh-faced and hearty.

One of the appeals of the breed is his medium-length, close, hard coat. But even a coat of that length needs regular brushing and bathing. A clean coat is a healthy coat. Bathing and brushing reduces shedding and keeps the coat shiny and pleasant-smelling. Besides, your dog will really appreciate the pampering and the special quality time you spend with him.

Grooming time is a great opportunity to go over your dog's body and look for any lumps, red or swollen areas, and fleas and ticks. Check, too, for any broken or cracked teeth or swollen gums. Catching these problems early on will help you get treatment for your dog and possibly avert a more serious problem. Don't hesitate to contact your veterinarian if you're concerned about any of these conditions.

Plan on hearing your Beagle howl a few *ah-roos* and watching him zip around the house when you finish the grooming routine. Being clean and fresh is so energizing! You'll appreciate your sweet-smelling dog even more the next time he snuggles up to you.

The First Grooming Session

Begin grooming your dog the day after you bring him home. Or, if you've had your dog for a while and have never paid much attention to his beauty needs, now's the time to start.

If your Beagle fusses and fidgets, be patient. It may take a few times to train him to stand still for his grooming session. Keep a lot of food treats on hand and be prepared to give him one every time he allows you to brush even a few strokes, so he'll begin to associate grooming with a positive experience. Once he figures out that being handled is a good thing, grooming will be a snap.

Don't try to do everything at your first session—brushing, bathing, trimming nails, cleaning ears and eyes, and brushing his teeth. Do one or two procedures, perhaps the bath and cleaning his ears, and just show your dog the toothbrush. This way, both of you won't feel overwhelmed.

To avoid a fuss, begin short grooming sessions with your dog right from the start.

Grooming Schedule

Bathing	Once a month
Brushing	Once or twice a week
Nail trimming	Once a week
Ear or eye cleaning	Once a week; daily if there's a problem
Dental care	Daily

For the next session, add a third procedure. It may take you and your dog a few sessions to feel comfortable enough to undergo all of the grooming tasks, but that's okay. You're setting a routine that you'll be able to maintain for the rest of your dog's life.

Choose a regular day and time for grooming, when you're not rushed. This way, you can take your time and even enjoy the process. Establishing a regular routine helps both of you adapt to the routine.

Grooming Supplies

Before grooming your dog, gather up all the things you'll need. Nothing is more frustrating than giving your dog a bath and realizing you forgot to get a towel! Here's a list of the things you'll need to keep your Beagle well groomed:

- Medium-bristle brush for routine brushing
- Undercoat shedding blade for removing undercoat during shedding season
- Fine-toothed flea comb to find fleas that might be hiding beneath the coat
- Spray bottle filled with water and two tablespoons of Listerine to give the coat a nice shine
- Non-skid mat for sink or bathtub
- Rubber brush for bathing
- Spray nozzle attachment for sink or tub
- Dog shampoo
- Towels for drying after a bath
- Canine toothbrush and canine toothpaste
- Nail clipper or cordless, battery-operated pet nail grinder
- Styptic powder or cornstarch for nail trimming; you only need a little container

- Ear-cleaning solution
- Cotton balls or gauze pads for cleaning ears and keeping them dry

Giving the Brush-Off

It takes only about fifteen minutes to brush a Beagle, but it should be done once or twice a week. This helps keep his coat and skin healthy. Brushing stimulates the pores and spreads the skin's natural oils throughout the coat. Frequent brushing also cuts down on shedding by getting rid of the dead hair and promoting new

Brush your dog once or twice a week to keep his skin and coat healthy.

T I P

When you groom your dog, instead of bending over him, put him up on a table. A grooming or picnic table works well, but any table will do. Put a rubber-backed plastic tablecloth or a bath mat on top of the table to keep your Beagle from sliding off. The job is so much easier when he's at your eye level. Be sure to keep one hand on him at all times so he doesn't fall off.

---

hair growth. It also gives the coat a healthy, glossy look.

A healthy Beagle coat shouldn't be dull and brittle or dry and flaky. If you notice these conditions, it could mean your dog has a thyroid condition, allergies, parasites, or a diet that's too low in fat.

Your Beagle should not have an odor, either. When people say Beagles are smelly, it's usually because they have known some who were never washed, brushed, or properly cared for. Unfortunately, some misinformed Beagle owners insist on keeping their hounds chained outside because they say that living in the house ruins them for hunting. This is totally unacceptable for any dog. Dogs are companion animals and need human interaction. They should live inside the house, whether they hunt or not.

Before brushing your dog, run the flea comb through your dog's body, legs, chest, neck, and head to pick up any fleas. When you think you've found them all, use the medium-bristle brush for serious brushing, although don't be surprised if a few more fleas pop up.

To brush your dog, start at the top of his head and work toward the tail. Don't forget to run the brush down his legs and chest and along his sides. Repeat the process a few times. If there's a lot of loose hair coming out, continue brushing a few minutes until the brush comes away almost clean.

When your dog begins to shed his winter coat in the warm weather, use the shedding blade after brushing. Beginning at the neck, gently run it through your Beagle's fur toward the tail. Don't use it on his face, because you can accidentally injure his eyes if you're too close.

When you're done brushing, use a damp towel to wipe him down. For a good shine to the coat, mix a little water with two or three tablespoons of Listerine and spray a little all over your dog. This will also make him smell clean and fresh.

A Good Soak

Beagles love to be adventuresome outdoors, and they're going to get a little dirty and grimy. Okay, maybe a lot dirty, but nothing that a good bath with some dog shampoo, water, and a light scrubbing won't fix. More than just making your dog smell good, bathing restores your dog's coat to a healthy condition.

Most Beagles love their bath.

Bathe your dog at least once a month, or more often if he gets into something that's really grubby. If your Beagle is mostly a television watcher, you can even bathe him once every six weeks.

Before starting the bath, put the bath mat in the bottom of the tub to prevent your dog from slipping and sliding. Next, place a cotton ball in each ear to keep the water out. Be sure to remember to take them out when you're done with the bath. Fill the tub with a little warm water and carefully put your dog in. Don't expect him to jump in, because he'll think you expect him to jump out again. He can also hit an elbow or leg on the edge of the tub and injure himself.

Wet him down and add a little shampoo on his back, chest, neck, and hindquarters. Don't use people shampoo on your dog! Canine shampoo has the correct pH for dogs and is specially formulated for their skin and coat. Use the rubber brush to work the soap into your dog's coat. You don't need a lot of lather to get the job done. A lot of shampoo just makes it more difficult to rinse all the soap out. To avoid eye irritation, keep the soap out of your dog's eyes. If some gets in, rinse his eyes immediately with water.

After soaping him up, use the spray nozzle attachment to rinse your dog thoroughly. This makes rinsing so much easier than having to fill a bucket with water, although if you don't have a spray nozzle, the bucket will work just fine. Just when you think you've gotten all the soap out, rinse him one more time. If you leave soap on his coat, you'll most likely see some dull flakes the next day. Place a towel over your dog the minute you take him out of the tub so he doesn't shake water everywhere. Towel him dry. This is the part of the bath your dog will no doubt love the best. Be sure to take the cotton balls out of his ears!

Dental Care

According to the American Veterinary Dental Society, 80 percent of dogs develop gum disease by the time they're 3 years old. Taking care of your dog's teeth now prevents long-term health problems. Dental disease can even affect the heart, kidneys, and liver.

It's not that hard to get your dog to accept toothbrushing if you start him out young.

If you have a puppy and you see a tooth or two lying around the house, though, don't worry. Dogs lose their baby teeth between 3 and 6 months of age. Puppies have twenty-eight teeth—six incisors on the upper jaw and six on the lower, two upper and two lower canines, and four premolars on the upper and lower jaws. Adults have forty-two teeth, which includes the new molars that erupt when dogs are 7 months old.

Use a canine toothbrush and canine toothpaste for your dog. There are many models to choose from—

Eye, Eye

Every once in a while your dog's eyes may have a slight clear discharge, especially after he wakes up from a nap. Wipe it away with a gauze pad or a facial tissue. If the discharge is yellow or greenish, if there is any swelling in the eye, or if he is blinking a lot or has difficulty opening his eye, he may have an eye infection. Take him to your veterinarian.

even a finger brush that works well. Unlike human toothpaste, the doggy toothpaste dissolves in your dog's mouth and doesn't need rinsing. Dogs like the taste, and it continues to clean your dog's teeth long after you've stopped brushing.

To begin brushing the teeth, show your puppy the toothbrush and paste the day after you bring him home, so he can become accustomed to it. Let him lick a little toothpaste off of your finger or rub it over one of his teeth. When he easily accepts your finger in his mouth, try putting the toothbrush in his mouth, even if just for a moment.

The next time, add some paste to the brush and brush one tooth. Continue to add a tooth or two each time you brush his teeth. You don't need to spend a lot of time doing this. A swipe or two across each puppy tooth is enough. He's going to lose these puppy teeth anyway, but you're just introducing the process so that when he has his adult teeth, he'll be comfortable with brushing.

Once the adult teeth come in, they should be brushed once a day. By brushing your dog's teeth daily and having your veterinarian check your dog's teeth during his regular checkup, you'll greatly reduce the chances that he'll develop dental disease later on.

Before brushing, look in your dog's mouth. His gums should be pink, not red or swollen. If something doesn't look right, contact your veterinarian.

Nail Salon

Dogs' nails grow. That happens no matter how much walking or running on cement they do or how much you trim them. Like people, some dogs just have longer nail beds than others, and the nails grow out faster and longer. You should

Get your dog used to having his paws handled before you start cutting his nails.

never let your dog's nails curl over his feet. This puts pressure on the feet and legs and leads to foot problems.

By trimming the nails regularly—preferably once a week—you can prevent nail trouble before it starts. Once you begin establishing a regular nail trimming routine, the job goes quickly.

Dog owners always dread cutting nails, mostly because they're afraid they'll hurt their dog by clipping off too much and the nail will bleed. So they neglect the job. While bleeding is always a possibility and occasionally it happens to even the most experienced groomers, the job still needs to be done. Like most things, the more you do it, the better you'll get. If a nail does bleed, dip it into a little styptic powder, which will stop the bleeding immediately.

If you have someone to help you the first few times, this makes clipping easier. But if not, you can still do the job yourself. To prepare your dog, make sure he's comfortable with you touching his feet. Some dogs will yelp if you even pick up a paw, so get him accustomed to you holding and rubbing his feet several times before you even pick up the clippers. You can do this while he's snuggling up against you or while he's taking a nap and you're both relaxed. When he doesn't fuss when you handle his feet, he's ready for his first pedicure.

The First Session

Keep small food treats close at hand and plan on giving your dog one after he lets you clip just one nail. Show your dog the clippers or electric nail grinder and let him sniff them and listen to the whirl of the grinder. Pick up a paw and, while holding it gently, trim off the tip of the nail where there is a slight hook. While the grinder can be a little noisy, you can be more accurate with it and not worry about slicing off too much of the nail. It takes a little longer to use than the clippers, but you'll be able to see a drop of blood and stop before there's more bleeding.

Avoid hitting the quick—the blood vessel inside—which is pink in light-colored toenails. With dark nails you can't see the quick, so just take off the pointed tip of the nail. If you see blood, put a little bit of styptic powder or cornstarch on the area to stop the bleeding. Just don't panic. Your dog isn't going to die if one toenail bleeds a little. Give him a food treat to reward him for trusting you.

Don't plan on doing all the nails at once. Just do a few the first time and add a few more at later sessions. Soon you'll be able to trim all your dog's nails quickly and efficiently.

If the whole process is more than you can truly manage, take your dog to a groomer to have the job done. The cost is usually minimal and your dog will have safe toenails.

The Ears Have It

Hanging Beagle ears definitely add to your dog's personality, but they do require more cleaning than ears that stand up. They wind up wet from the water dish, and because they cover the ear opening and prevent air from circulating, Beagles can be more prone to ear infections. Check your dog's ears once a week, or even once a day if he's having problems, to make sure there isn't an odor. A musty smell signals a waxy buildup and that it's time for an ear cleaning.

If you see your dog shaking his head, scratching his ears, or rubbing his head on the ground, it may mean an ear infection. Your veterinarian can examine your dog's ears and recommend the right treatment. Ask him or her to demonstrate the best way to clean the ears.

To keep your dog still during a routine ear cleaning, ask someone to help hold him for you. If no one's available, snap on his leash and sit on a portion of it while you clean.

Begin by putting a few drops of the liquid ear cleaner into the opening of one of your dog's ears and gently massage the ear back and forth to work the solution down

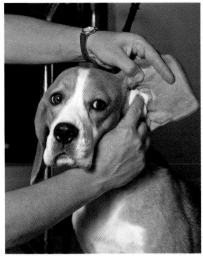

Those houndy ears need to be routinely cleaned. Make sure you don't push the cotton balls into the dog's ear canal.

into the canal. Quickly put a cotton ball into the opening and wipe around the inside as far as the cotton will reach before he has a chance to shake his head. Don't worry. You can't hurt the ear drum because a dog's ear drum is halfway down his neck! (Still, don't push the cotton onto the ear canal.) If the cotton comes out dirty, insert drops again and wipe out the ear a few more times until the cotton comes out clean. Repeat the process with the other ear. When you're done, give your dog a treat.

Getting Rid of Pests

Depending on where you live, there's always the chance that your dog may give a tick or a flea a free ride. Some wooded areas, particularly where Beagles like to go exploring and hunting, are huge flea and tick communities. One of the many advantages of weekly grooming is that you can spot the varmints before they set up housekeeping on your dog.

If you discover even one pest, there are more waiting in the wings, since they always travel with friends. The average life span of a flea is two weeks to eight months, and they thrive in warm temperatures. One female can lay 15 to 20 eggs a day and up to 600 during her lifetime.

Fleas will make an adult dog itchy and miserable. But they're even worse for a puppy, who can get seriously ill from an infestation.

New Products in the Fight Against Fleas

At one time, battling fleas meant exposing your dog and yourself to toxic dips, sprays, powders, and collars. But today there are flea preventives that work very well and are safe for your dog, you, and the environment. The two most common types are insect growth regulators (IGRs), which stop the immature flea from developing or maturing, and adult flea killers. To deal with an active infestation, experts usually recommend a product that has both.

These next-generation flea fighters generally come in one of two forms:

- **Topical treatments or spot-ons.** These products are applied to the skin, usually between the shoulder blades. The product is absorbed through the skin into the dog's system.
- **Systemic products.** This is a pill your dog swallows that transmits a chemical throughout the dog's bloodstream. When a flea bites the dog, it picks up this chemical, which then prevents the flea's eggs from developing.

Talk to your veterinarian about which product is best for your dog. Make sure you read all the labels and apply the products exactly as recommended, and that you check to make sure they are safe for puppies.

The sooner you can get rid of them, the better. It takes only one flea or tick to harm your dog's health. Besides irritating your dog, fleas can cause an allergic reaction that can be lethal for some dogs. Fleas also transmit tapeworm and other illnesses that can really harm your dog. Ticks also carry some very nasty diseases. Therefore, take all of the steps necessary to prevent them from moving in on your dog. The effort is worth it.

Making Your Environment Flea Free

If there are fleas on your dog, there are fleas in your home, yard, and car, even if you can't see them. Take these steps to combat them.

In your home:

- Wash whatever is washable (the dog bed, sheets, blankets, pillow covers, slipcovers, curtains, etc. . .).
- Vacuum everything else in your home—furniture, floors, rugs, everything. Pay special attention to the folds and crevices in upholstery, the cracks between floorboards, and the spaces between the floor and the baseboards. Flea larvae are sensitive to sunlight, so inside the house they prefer deep carpet, bedding, and cracks and crevices.
- When you're done, throw the vacuum cleaner bag away—in an outside garbage can.
- Use a nontoxic flea-killing powder to treat your carpets (but remember, it does not control fleas elsewhere in the house). The powder stays deep in the carpet and kills fleas (using a form of boric acid) for up to a year.
- If you have a particularly serious flea problem, consider using a fogger or long-lasting spray to kill any adult and larval fleas, or having a professional exterminator treat your home.

Fleas

On a tri-color Beagle coat, it's not always easy to spot a black flea because they're in camouflage gear. To look for fleas on your dog, examine his coat in bright light. To find fleas easily, comb your dog with a fine-toothed flea comb. They usually show up around the tail, hips, and belly, but don't be surprised if you see one or more on his head and chest. Pick them up when you see them and dump them into a bowl of hot water, where they will die.

Follow the instructions in the boxes above and on page 77 to get rid of fleas on your dog and in your home.

In your car:

- Take out the floor mats and hose them down with a strong stream of water, then hang them up to dry in the sun.
- Wash any towels, blankets, or other bedding you regularly keep in the car.
- Thoroughly vacuum the entire interior of your car, paying special attention to the seams between the bottom and back of the seats.
- When you're done, throw the vacuum cleaner bag away—in an outside garbage can.

In your yard:

- Flea larvae prefer shaded areas that have plenty of organic material and moisture, so rake the yard thoroughly and bag all the debris in tightly sealed bags.
- Spray your yard with an insecticide that has residual activity for at least thirty days. Insecticides that use a form of boric acid are nontoxic. Some products contain an insect growth regulator (such as fenoxycarb) and need to be applied only once or twice a year.
- For an especially difficult flea problem, consider having an exterminator treat your yard.
- Keep your yard free of piles of leaves, weeds, and other organic debris. Be especially careful in shady, moist areas, such as under bushes.

Ticks

By grooming your dog regularly, you'll be able to detect any ticks before they have a chance to harm your dog. Ticks carry Lyme disease, Rocky Mountain spotted fever, and other ailments that are dangerous to both people and dogs.

Look for poppy seed–size immature ticks or sesame seed–size adults. Ticks are brown or black and are not always easy to find on a tri-color Beagle, but look anyway. If you find a tick clinging to your dog, carefully remove it immediately by following the directions in the box on page 80. Don't touch it with your fingers because it can bite and infect you.

How to Get Rid of a Tick

Although many of the new generation of flea fighters are partially effective in killing ticks once they are on your dog, they are not 100 percent effective and will not keep ticks from biting your dog in the first place. During tick season (which, depending on where you live, can be spring, summer, and/or fall), examine your dog every day for ticks. Pay particular attention to your dog's neck, behind the ears, the armpits, and the groin.

When you find a tick, use a pair of tweezers to grasp the tick as close as possible to the dog's skin and pull it out using firm, steady pressure. Check to make sure you get the whole tick (mouth parts left in your dog's skin can cause an infection), then wash the wound and dab it with a little antibiotic ointment. Watch for signs of inflammation.

Ticks carry very serious diseases that are transmittable to humans, so dispose of the tick safely. *Never* crush it between your fingers. Don't flush it down the toilet either, because the tick will survive the trip and infect another animal. Instead, use the tweezers to place the tick in a tight-sealing jar or plastic dish with a little alcohol, put on the lid, and dispose of the container in an outdoor garbage can. Wash the tweezers thoroughly with hot water and alcohol.

Chapter 8

Keeping Your Beagle Healthy

The Beagle is a low-maintenance, remarkably hardy little hound, with a lusty appetite and an activity level that varies from dog to dog. She is typically carefree and not prone to anxiety or neuroses. All these things contribute to the basic good health of the breed. With relatively few hereditary problems, quality veterinary care, regular grooming, and a nutritious and healthy diet, she should live a long and happy life.

Choosing Your Veterinarian

You should choose a veterinarian with the same kind of care you take in selecting your family physician. Veterinarians have different personalities, treatment philosophies, specializations, and office practices. Your veterinarian should be a professional you feel comfortable talking with, someone who never rushes you. These factors determine how effective your relationship will be in the years ahead with your Beagle.

Even if your Beagle is healthy throughout her entire life, she will still need to see the veterinarian to be spayed and for regular checkups. So you should like her veterinarian. To find a good veterinarian, contact the American Animal Hospital Association (listed in the appendix), or ask your puppy's breeder, other friends with dogs, the breed rescue coordinator, or the local animal shelter for recommendations.

To make the final decision, call the vet's office and ask if you can schedule an appointment to tour the office and meet with the veterinarian for a few minutes, with or without your dog. You should expect to pay for this time. This gives you

Your veterinarian will be your partner in your dog's health for the rest of your Beagle's life. Take the time to carefully choose a veterinarian.

a chance to see how clean the facilities are and the opportunity to chat with the vet before there's a problem with your dog.

Interviewing Veterinarians

You'll be asking a lot of questions, and that's okay. If your dog ever gets sick, you'll want to know who you're dealing with. Inquire about the veterinarian's credentials—what veterinary school they graduated from and if they have a specialty. Ask if they see other Beagles in their practice and what some of the breed problems are. Although it's nice to have a vet who sees a lot of Beagles, it's not a must. A good veterinarian knows about hounds and keeps up with the latest health developments.

Ask about other veterinarians on the staff and if you can request the same doctor each time. It's good to see the same vet as often as possible, so they really get to know your dog. But if there's more than one veterinarian in the office, you'll be able to see a doctor when you need one.

Find out what the office hours are and what happens if there's an emergency after hours. Do they want you to call them or should you take your dog to an emergency animal clinic? Know what the procedure is before you need to use it.

You'll want to find a veterinary clinic that's clean, knowledgeable, friendly, helpful, and genuinely likes dogs. Look for that special home-away-from-home feeling where you just know that your dog is being well taken care of.

The veterinarian should always explain medical information in terms you can easily understand, be patient with your questions, and like your dog. You should never feel rushed and always feel comfortable talking with the veterinarian. If, at any time, you don't like the way the veterinarian speaks to you, it doesn't matter what their credentials are or who recommended them—they're not the veterinarian for you.

Holistic Options

Holistic medicine is a combination of alternative treatments, such as acupuncture, chiropractic care, and botanical and homeopathic remedies. According to the American Holistic Veterinary Medical Association (AHVMA), holistic techniques are gentle, minimally invasive, and incorporate patient well-being and stress reduction. To find holistic veterinarians, contact the AHVMA (listed in the appendix).

Some veterinarians combine conventional and alternative methods. When qualified veterinarians use holistic and conventional methods, they can offer your Beagle a full range of treatment possibilities. There are times when some dog owners are willing to try anything that will help their dogs live a longer life.

The First Visit

Take your Beagle to the veterinarian two or three days after you first bring her home. Your dog may seem healthy to you, but a veterinarian may spot something you will miss. The veterinarian should listen to your dog's heart and lungs, take her temperature, weigh her, and examine her coat, skin, eyes, ears, feet, and mouth. Bring along a fresh stool sample that will reveal whether your dog has any internal parasites.

Tell the doctor what kind of food your dog is eating, how much and how often you're feeding her, and whether you have any questions or problems.

Talk about an overall healthcare plan for your Beagle. This should include flea, tick, and heartworm preventives, when to spay her (or neuter him), when she needs to return to the office for vaccines, and, if you have a puppy, when to change her diet from a puppy recipe to an adult one.

Preventive Care

Your veterinarian will want to monitor your dog's health by seeing her for a routine checkup once a year. Sometimes it may not seem like your Beagle needs to see the doctor, but a lot can happen in a dog's life in twelve months.

The annual checkup monitors your dog's overall health. Your veterinarian can detect any problems with her skin, eyes, teeth, heart, kidneys, or liver. As your

Beagle ages, there's a chance that she may develop cancer or skin or eye problems, and your veterinarian may be able to spot these early on.

In addition to regular checkups, there are other preventive measures you can take to ensure your Beagle's health.

Fence Her In

Many Beagle rescue organizations require owners to have a securely fenced yard. There's a very good reason for this. Beagles have been selectively bred for hundreds of years to follow a scent trail. When they catch a scent, their noses hit the ground and they follow that scent anywhere. This is pure instinct.

Your dog should have a wellness check a few days after you bring her home.

You can call several times, but chances are your Beagle will not listen and will not come back. It's not that she doesn't love you and wants to run away or that she is being purposely disobedient. She's just following her nose. That's the job of a Beagle. We humans, as their guardians, need to make sure they are safely contained so that their noses don't get them into trouble.

After-Exercise Check

If you hunt with your Beagle, check her over for signs of any injuries when you get home. Perhaps she's stepped on a thorn or has a cut ear that can worsen if not properly taken care of right away. Weed seeds or other foreign objects can also find their way into her eyes. Flush her eyes out with water or a saline solution to reduce irritation.

After hunting, give your Beagle a good brushing, too. This will help locate and dislodge any burrs or thorns that may have found their way into the skin and could become dangerous.

Monitor Food and Weight

Feeding is the cornerstone of a sound healthcare program for your Beagle. The old Irish admonition that hounds should be fed when they're hungry and not

Why Spay and Neuter?

Breeding dogs is a serious undertaking that should only be part of a well-planned breeding program. Why? Because dogs pass on their physical and behavioral problems to their offspring. Even healthy, well-behaved dogs can pass on problems in their genes.

Is your dog so sweet that you'd like to have a litter of puppies just like her? If you breed her to another dog, the pups will not have the same genetic heritage she has. Breeding her *parents* again will increase the odds of a similar pup, but even then, the puppies in the second litter could inherit different genes. In fact, *there is no way to breed a dog to be just like another dog*.

Meanwhile, thousands and thousands of dogs are killed in animal shelters every year simply because they have no homes. Casual breeding is a big contributor to this problem.

If you don't plan to breed your dog, is it still a good idea to spay her or neuter him? Yes!

When you spay your female:

- You avoid her heat cycles, during which she discharges blood and scent.
- It greatly reduces the risk of mammary cancer and eliminates the risk of pyometra (an often fatal infection of the uterus) and uterine cancer.
- It prevents unwanted pregnancies.
- It reduces dominance behaviors and aggression.

When you neuter your male:

- It curbs the desire to roam and to fight with other males.
- It greatly reduces the risk of prostate cancer and eliminates the risk of testicular cancer.
- It helps reduce leg lifting and mounting behavior.
- It reduces dominance behaviors and aggression.

Keep your dog at a good weight to ensure her long-term health.

have food lying around all day is good advice. When you control how much your Beagle eats at each meal and you consistently give her high-quality food, she will want to eat at meal times. She will not become a picky eater.

Don't give your Beagle table scraps if she doesn't eat her regular food. If you do, you'll never know whether she is ill or just being picky.

Internal Parasites

Internal parasites include worms and protozoa. Some parasites show up in the dog's stool, while others show no outward signs. You won't know that your dog has them until you notice that she has lost a lot of weight despite a very healthy appetite, or she has an unusually rounded abdomen. Other symptoms include a lackluster coat, dull eyes, weakness, coughing, vomiting, and diarrhea.

If you suspect your dog has parasites, take a fresh stool sample to your veterinarian for analysis. Even if you don't think your puppy has parasites, it's a good idea to have her stool checked at her first veterinary visit, just to make sure. If she does have parasites, your veterinarian can prescribe medication to rid your dog of these nasty pests.

Picking up stools frequently and keeping the Beagle's living area clean helps prevent further problems.

Worms

What we commonly call worms are parasites ranging in size from less than an inch to several feet long. They may be nothing more than a nuisance, or they can be life-threatening. Generally speaking, puppies or older or weak animals are more susceptible to illness as a result of a parasite infestation. It is better to prevent or treat early than to wait until the dog is weakened. A number of internal parasites may infect dogs, but the most common are roundworms, hookworms, tapeworms, whipworms, and heartworms.

Heartworms

Heartworms colonize the circulatory system rather than the digestive system. This parasite is spread by mosquitoes and is a problem all over the country. Part of your dog's routine care will be an annual test for the presence of these silent killers before putting her on preventive medication. In some areas, veterinarians recommend keeping dogs on heartworm preventives year-round.

With new medications that need to be administered only once a month and which often help control other parasites as well, this disease is easily prevented. A cure for the infected dog is another matter. Since the worms, often up to twelve inches long, cluster in the heart, too abrupt a death of these creatures can cause blockage and death. Also, the agents used to kill the worms are fairly toxic, so you need to avoid these threats to your Beagle's life.

Parasites lurk everywhere in the great outdoors. Beagles, who often have their nose on the ground, can pick up parasite eggs from the soil.

Vaccines

What vaccines dogs need and how often they need them has been a subject of controversy for several years. Researchers, health care professionals, vaccine manufacturers, and dog owners do not always agree on which vaccines each dog needs or how often booster shots must be given.

In 2006, the American Animal Hospital Association issued a set of vaccination guidelines and recommendations intended to help dog owners and veterinarians sort through much of the controversy and conflicting information. The guidelines designate four vaccines as core, or essential for every dog, because of the serious nature of the diseases and their widespread distribution. These are canine distemper virus (using a modified live virus or recombinant modified live virus vaccine), canine parvovirus (using a modified live virus vaccine), canine adenovirus-2 (using a modified live virus vaccine), and rabies (using a killed virus). The general recommendations for their administration (except rabies, for which you must follow local laws) are:

- Vaccinate puppies at 6–8 weeks, 9–11 weeks, and 12–14 weeks.
- Give an initial "adult" vaccination when the dog is older than 16 weeks; two doses, three to four weeks apart, are

Giardia

This single-celled parasite is a huge nuisance. Transmitted through contaminated drinking water, the signs of giardia are light-colored, foul smelling, and mucousy or bloody stool. Your veterinarian can diagnose it only by examining a stool sample. Medication can ease the discomfort.

advised, but one dose is considered protective and
acceptable.

- Give a booster shot when the dog is 1 year old.
- Give a subsequent booster shot every three years, unless
  there are risk factors that make it necessary to vaccinate
  more or less often.

Noncore vaccines should only be considered for those dogs
who risk exposure to a particular disease because of geographic
area, lifestyle, frequency of travel, or other issues. They include
vaccines against distemper-measles virus, canine parainfluenza
virus, leptospirosis, Bordetella bronchiseptica, and Borrelia
burgdorferi (Lyme disease).

Vaccines that are not generally recommended because the
disease poses little risk to dogs or is easily treatable, or the vaccine has not been proven to be effective, are those against giardia, canine coronavirus, and canine adenovirus-1.

Often, combination injections are given to puppies, with one
shot containing several core and noncore vaccines. Your veterinarian may be reluctant to use separate shots that do not include
the noncore vaccines, because they must be specially ordered. If
you are concerned about these noncore vaccines, talk to your vet.

Coccidia

When dogs are kept in crowded conditions, they're liable to contract coccidia,
an intestinal parasite. Highly contagious coccidia is transmitted through
contaminated food or water and causes bloating, bloody stool, straining during
elimination, vomiting, and weight loss.

Heartworms live everywhere mosquitoes live. It's easier to prevent them than it is to treat an infestation.

To keep this nasty parasite off your premises, promptly clean up feces and clean the kennel area or spray the yard with an antiseptic solution.

Beagle Health Problems

Beagles as a breed don't have many health problems, but no breed is completely free from every health issue. National Beagle Club members are knowledgeable about the breed's health issues, and they work to educate Beagle breeders and owners about their prevalence. When you are purchasing a Beagle from a breeder, ask if the dog's parents have passed health clearances for hip dysplasia from the Orthopedic Foundation for Animals (OFA) and have eye tests from the Canine Eye Registration Foundation (CERF).

Bleeding Disorders

If a Beagle bleeds easily and continues to bleed after getting a little nick or cut, she may have hemophilia A. This is a bleeding disorder that occurs when there is a deficiency in a specific clotting factor known as factor VIII.

Both purebred and mixed breed dogs can suffer from hemophilia. Beagles with mild forms of it may have few or no signs, or may never require treatment unless they have excessive bleeding following surgery.

In severe cases, a puppy may have prolonged bleeding after losing a baby tooth; bleeding into muscles or joints can cause lameness. Your veterinarian can diagnose the condition and suggest ways to manage it.

Cancer

When a dog is diagnosed with cancer, it's frightening. The thought of losing a cherished Beagle is devastating. Nearly every breed and mixed breed is stricken by cancer. Statistics reveal that one in five dogs will develop it. Fortunately, veterinary oncologists know more about fighting this disease than ever before, and dogs respond very well to the numerous types of treatments if the cancer is discovered early enough.

A very subtle change in behavior can often be the only sign of a health problem. Get to know your Beagle, and when things are "just not right," take her to the vet.

Cherry Eye

Cherry Eye is the infection and swelling of the third eyelid in dogs. It's common in Beagles and may be treated with a simple surgical procedure or may even respond to antibiotics. With the redness and swelling, the condition looks a lot worse than it is; many animals don't seem to know there is a problem.

It's caused when one of the tear-producing glands located at the inner corner of the eye slips. This can occur in one or both eyes, and not always at the same time. Puppies can develop it seemingly overnight.

Chondrodystrophy

Also known as dwarfism or skeletal dysplasia, chondrodystrophy is the disease responsible for keeping a Beagle small, deformed, and in constant leg and joint pain. It first shows

---

TIP

Applying Eye Ointment

Since Beagles are prone to cherry eye, you'll probably be applying eye ointment to your dog's eyes a few times throughout her life. It's easy to do, so don't worry. Hold your dog's head and lift one edge of the eyelid. Squeeze the tube slightly into the pocket between the lower lid and the eye. If she blinks, that's okay. The ointment should spread into the eye automatically.

up at 3 to 4 weeks of age and prevents the bones and vertebrae from growing properly.

If a breeder tries to convince you that an undersized Beagle is really a rare Pocket Beagle and is perfectly healthy, run the other way. This puppy will limp when she walks and will always need special care.

By the time the pup's growth plates close at around 4 months of age, the bones have closed and her legs may be crooked. There is no cure but there are medications available that will ease the pain.

Ear Mites

Ear mites are probably present in most mature Beagles kept in kennels. Why they become a problem for some hounds and not others is a mystery, but when they cause an infection, they make a dog miserable. The Beagle will scratch at the inside of her ear and constantly shake her head. Secondary bacterial or fungal infections can develop.

If you clean your dog's ears regularly, she shouldn't have mites. This is another example of an ounce of prevention being worth a pound of cure. Your veterinarian will check your hound's ears as part of her regular checkup. If you don't already know how to do it, ask your veterinarian how to properly clean your dog's ears.

Epilepsy

Epileptic seizures appear in some Beagle families. The degree of severity can range from the *petit mal* form, which may be nothing more than the dog "spacing out" for a few minutes, to *grand mal*, which involves loss of muscular control, stiffening, and convulsions. *Grand mal* seizures may last several minutes, during which time you are convinced your dog is going to die. When the seizure is over, the dog appears subdued or disoriented for a few more minutes and then acts as if nothing ever happened. Mild forms present no major problems for the average house dog, but the more serious forms require medication.

Another closely related condition in Beagles is known as running fits. These occur when the hound is hunting and suddenly runs off as if she is being chased by the devil himself! Internal parasites, nutritional deficiencies, or low blood sugar may be responsible, but no one knows the exact cause.

Glaucoma

Glaucoma is one of the major reasons dogs go blind. Signs include red eyes, tearing, sensitivity to light, and enlargement of the eye. The eye may look glassy or the pupil may be unusually dilated. This condition is caused by fluid pressure

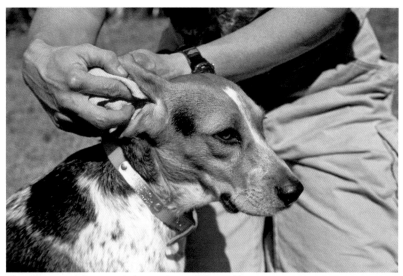

If you clean your dog's ears regularly, ear mites won't be a problem.

inside the eye because the fluid does not drain properly. Treatment can help if a diagnosis is made early enough. Blindness results if there is no treatment.

Heart Disease

Beagles can suffer from a few heart problems: pulmonic stenosis, dilated cardiomyopathy, and ventricular septal defect. There are good treatments available for these conditions, and veterinary researchers are always learning more. To locate a veterinary cardiologist in your area, contact the American College of Veterinary Internal Medicine (listed in the appendix).

Pulmonic stenosis is a narrowing of the connection between the right ventricle and the pulmonary artery. The right ventricle has a hard time pumping blood, causing the right side of the heart to become enlarged.

Dilated cardiomyopathy is an enlarged heart; it's a common cause of congestive heart failure. The signs include shortness of breath, blue gums or a blue tongue after exercise, lack of stamina, coughing, lack of appetite, and weight loss. Early detection is important to control this condition with medication.

When a Beagle is born with ventricular septal defect (a small hole in the wall of her heart), it may not cause much of a problem other than poor circulation. A larger hole may be more serious, forcing the heart to work too hard.

Like all breeds, Beagles can suffer from a number of inherited health problems. A reputable breeder will know what these are and will take steps to make sure they produce healthy puppies.

Hip Dysplasia

This painful condition can lead to crippling arthritis. Present at birth, hip dysplasia is an abnormal formation of the hip socket where the head of the femur (thigh bone) does not fit snugly into the pelvis, eventually resulting in lameness.

When choosing dogs to breed, breeders should have both males and females X-rayed after the age of 2 years, when the bones have fully formed, to detect the presence or absence of this abnormality. Dogs who are severely affected (dysplastic) and do not pass minimum standards for a tight fit should not be bred.

Hot Spots

Hot spots are warm, itchy, swollen patches of skin. Hair in the area is quickly lost. The infection progresses when the dog licks and chews the site. The resulting lesion is raw-looking and moist. The causes of this condition are unclear. Treatment usually involves anti-inflammatory agents to reduce the itching and prevent further skin damage and secondary infection.

Hypothyroidism

This is a common endocrine disorder among Beagles in which the thyroid does not produce enough hormones. Signs include hair loss, dry and scaly skin, sudden weight gain, flea and food allergies, and ear infections. With some mild cases these signs are barely noticeable. A simple blood test can detect the presence of hypothyroidism, and medication can help rebalance the dog's system.

Intervertebral Disc Disease

Intervertebral disc disease (IVDD) affects many Beagles and causes sudden, severe pain that can be crippling or deadly to your dog. It usually happens late in a Beagle's life or when a dog is very overweight, but it can also strike dogs as young as 1 year old. A dog who suddenly yelps when she tries to climb stairs or won't jump on or off the furniture may have IVDD.

When the discs between the vertebrae begin to dehydrate, they become brittle and lose their flexibility. You can sometimes feel them sticking out along your dog's back. If they stick out or rupture, they exert pressure on the spinal column, paralyzing the dog. This can happen in the neck, chest, or lower back.

Your veterinarian can confirm the diagnosis. In some cases the dog can improve with medication, but surgery may be needed for severe cases.

Patella Luxation

Also known as dislocated kneecaps, this happens when the patella (kneecap) slips in and out of the groove at the lower end of the femur (the large bone in the thigh). This health problem causes limping that ranges from slight to severe.

Your veterinarian or a veterinary orthopedic physician can X-ray the dog's kneecaps and diagnose the problem according to how severe the defect is. This information can be registered with the Orthopedic Foundation of America (OFA), although registration is optional. Surgery can correct serious abnormalities. It is not recommended for more mild ones because the dog will probably not feel pain except when she jumps. Lifestyle accommodation, such as doggy stairs to get on the furniture, can help.

Orthopedic problems can prevent your dog from enjoying an active life. Ask the breeder about what screening they do for these kinds of health problems.

Common Canine Health Problems

There are a few health problems that affect most dogs at some time in their lives. It's important to know what's serious and what's not. If you're ever in doubt, call the veterinarian.

Appetite Loss

Beagles love to eat, so if yours misses a meal or two and is active and drinking a normal amount of water, it's possible there's a health problem. If she misses a third meal, give the veterinarian a call. This isn't normal for a Beagle.

Coughing

Dogs cough. Maybe your Beagle swallowed something that didn't quite go down right or her throat is a little dry. If she has a persistent cough or intermittent gagging, she may have a respiratory infection and needs to see the veterinarian.

Diarrhea

Diarrhea by itself is a symptom rather than an illness and may be treated symptomatically, but remember that the cause must be addressed as well. Pepto-Bismol or Kaopectate may be used to treat the symptomatic diarrhea, and hamburger and boiled rice may be substituted for your hound's regular diet until things have calmed down.

If you can't clear up the problem with these remedies in a day or two, contact your veterinarian. Diarrhea that continues after two days may mean that something more serious is going on.

Impacted Anal Glands

Dogs who are not overweight, receive regular exercise, have enough fiber in their diets, and have normal, firm stools should not have a problem with their anal glands. These glands are located on either side of the anus and are related to the scent glands on skunks and foxes. If your dog has ever been badly frightened and you have noted an unpleasant odor, it's because these glands have emptied.

If your dog is licking or biting at her anal region or scooting her rear along the ground, it may mean she has impacted anal glands.

Before you ask your veterinarian whether your dog needs to have them emptied, try adding about a tablespoon of plain canned pumpkin (not pumpkin pie mix) to her food twice a day for a few days. In about a day or two, she should stop

Your dog is relying on you to know when a visit to the veterinarian is necessary. If there's any doubt, go to the vet.

scooting on the ground. If not, call your veterinarian.

After the glands are clear, add more fiber to your dog's diet, have her lose a few pounds, and take her out for more exercise.

Vomiting

If your dog vomits once or even twice, you probably don't have to worry. Sometimes your Beagle drinks too much water, has been chewing sharp blades of grass, or has eaten something that doesn't agree with her.

Skip her regular meal and instead give her a small amount of boiled rice and cottage cheese or boneless chicken for one or two meals. If that stays down, mix in a little of her regular food at the next meal.

If she vomits again or has diarrhea in the same day, contact your veterinarian.

It's an Emergency!

Don't wait until your dog has an emergency to read this information. Review it before your dog has a problem, so if she does need emergency care you'll know what to do. There are canine first-aid classes available that are worth taking. What you learn there may save your dog's life someday.

If your dog has any of these problems, don't wait. Call the veterinarian and let the office know that you're on the way. If your dog can't move, wrap her in a blanket and take her to the veterinarian immediately. Also make sure you know the phone number and location of the nearest 24-hour emergency clinic.

Bleeding

If you can stop the bleeding by applying direct pressure to the wound with your fingers or a towel, your dog should be okay. If the bleeding continues, take your dog to the veterinarian immediately.

When to Call the Veterinarian

Go to the vet right away or take your dog to an emergency veterinary clinic if:
- Your dog is choking
- Your dog is having trouble breathing
- Your dog has been injured and you cannot stop the bleeding within a few minutes
- Your dog has been stung or bitten by an insect and the site is swelling
- Your dog has been bitten by a snake
- Your dog has been bitten by another animal (including a dog) and shows any swelling or bleeding
- Your dog has touched, licked, or in any way been exposed to poison
- Your dog has been burned by either heat or caustic chemicals
- Your dog has been hit by a car
-

Your dog has been injured and is still limping an hour later

Broken Bones

Beagles are fairly well coordinated and don't usually run into things they shouldn't, but occasionally there's a Beagle who tries to jump over the three-foot retaining wall and craackk! If she's broken a bone, you'll probably know it. Instantly she won't be able to move and may scream in pain every time you try to move her.

Don't try to wrap the bone in a splint. Just transport her to the veterinarian right away.

Choking

If your dog is chewing on something and it doesn't go down, it can remain lodged in her throat and block her airway. If you see your dog gagging, pawing at her mouth, rubbing her face on the ground, or gasping for breath, she's choking.

- Your dog has unexplained swelling or redness
- Your dog's appetite changes
- Your dog vomits repeatedly and can't seem to keep food down, or drools excessively while eating
- You see any changes in your dog's urination or defecation (pain during elimination, change in regular habits, blood in urine or stool, diarrhea, foul-smelling stool)
- Your dog scoots her rear end on the floor
- Your dog's energy level, attitude, or behavior changes for no apparent reason
- Your dog has crusty or cloudy eyes, or excessive tearing or discharge
- Your dog's nose is dry or chapped, hot, crusty, or runny
- Your dog's ears smell foul, have a dark discharge, or seem excessively waxy
- Your dog's gums are inflamed or bleeding, her teeth look brown, or her breath is foul
- Your dog's skin is red, flaky, itchy, or inflamed, or she keeps chewing at certain spots
- Your dog's coat is dull, dry, brittle, or bare in spots
- Your dog's paws are red, swollen, tender, cracked, or the nails are split or too long
- Your dog is panting excessively, wheezing, unable to catch her breath, breathing heavily, or sounds strange when she breathes

Don't try to open her mouth and remove the blockage with your fingers, because she may accidentally bite you. The quickest and safest way to remove anything in your dog's throat is to try the Heimlich maneuver.

Place your arm around the dog's chest between the lower abdomen and the rib cage. Form a fist and bring your other hand around and cover your fist with it. Quickly thrust your two-handed fist inward and upward. Repeat several times until you have dislodged the object. If that doesn't work, transport your dog to the veterinarian's office.

Heatstroke

Heatstroke occurs if your dog overexercises in the heat of the day, is left in a kennel with no shade or water, or is left in a closed car when it's warm out. The interior of a car heats up quickly when the windows are shut, even if it's not all that

How to Make a Canine First-Aid Kit

If your dog hurts herself, even a minor cut, it can be very upsetting for both of you. Having a first-aid kit handy will help you to help her, calmly and efficiently. What should be in your canine first-aid kit?

- Antibiotic ointment
- Antiseptic and antibacterial cleansing wipes
- Benadryl
- Cotton-tipped applicators
- Disposable razor
- Elastic wrap bandages
- Extra leash and collar
- First-aid tape of various widths
- Gauze bandage roll
- Gauze pads of different sizes, including eye pads
- Hydrogen peroxide
- Instant cold compress
- Kaopectate or Pepto-Bismol tablets or liquid
- Latex gloves
- Lubricating jelly
- Muzzle
- Nail clippers
- Pen, pencil, and paper for notes and directions
- Plastic syringe with no needle (for administering liquids)
- Round-ended scissors and pointy scissors
- Safety pins
- Sterile saline eyewash
- Thermometer (rectal)
- Tweezers

hot outside. Leaving the windows open a crack doesn't help. It will be heartbreaking to return from shopping on a day in the 70s to find your Beagle dead.

A dog suffering from heatstroke has an elevated body temperature, is panting loudly, and her tongue and gums are bright red. Emergency treatment involves cooling her off as quickly as possible, including submerging her in cold water.

Make sure your pet is protected from extreme temperatures and always has plenty of cool, fresh water. That's the best prevention for heatstroke.

Poisoning

If your Beagle ingests or inhales a poisonous substance, she may have a seizure, begin vomiting, or have trouble breathing. Diarrhea, pain, lack of coordination, and foul-smelling breath or body odor are other signs of poisoning.

Beagles, who are so naturally active, may not know when they've had enough exercise on a hot day. Watch your dog carefully for signs of overheating.

Contact the ASPCA Animal Poison Control Center hotline (see the box below), then take her to your veterinarian or emergency clinic immediately!

ASPCA Animal Poison Control Center

The ASPCA Animal Poison Control Center has a staff of licensed veterinarians and board-certified toxicologists available 24 hours a day, 365 days a year. The number to call is (888)426-4435. You will be charged a consultation fee of $60 per case, charged to most major credit cards. There is no charge for follow-up calls in critical cases. At your request, they will also contact your veterinarian. Specific treatment and information can be provided via fax.

Keep the poison control number in large, legible print with your other emergency telephone numbers. When you call, be prepared to give your name, address, and phone number; what your dog has gotten into (the amount and how long ago); your dog's breed, age, sex, and weight; and what signs and symptoms the dog is showing. You can log onto www.aspca.org and click on "Animal Poison Control Center" for more information, including a list of toxic and nontoxic plants

Part III

Enjoying
Your Beagle

Chapter 9

Training Your Beagle

by Peggy Moran

Training makes your best friend better! A properly trained dog has a happier life and a longer life expectancy. He is also more appreciated by the people he encounters each day, both at home and out and about.

A trained dog walks nicely and joins his family often, going places untrained dogs cannot go. He is never rude or unruly, and he always happily comes when called. When he meets people for the first time, he greets them by sitting and waiting to be petted, rather than jumping up. At home he doesn't compete with his human family, and alone he is not destructive or overly anxious. He isn't continually nagged with words like "no," since he has learned not to misbehave in the first place. He is never shamed, harshly punished, or treated unkindly, and he is a well-loved, involved member of the family.

Sounds good, doesn't it? If you are willing to invest some time, thought, and patience, the words above could soon be used to describe your dog (though perhaps changing "he" to "she"). Educating your pet in a positive way is fun and easy, and there is no better gift you can give your pet than the guarantee of improved understanding and a great relationship.

This chapter will explain how to offer kind leadership, reshape your pet's behavior in a positive and practical way, and even get a head start on simple obedience training.

Understanding Builds the Bond

Dog training is a learning adventure on both ends of the leash. Before attempting to teach their dog new behaviors or change unwanted ones, thoughtful dog owners take the time to understand why their pets behave the way they do, and how their own behavior can be either a positive or negative influence on their dog.

Canine Nature

Loving dogs as much as we do, it's easy to forget they are a completely different species. Despite sharing our homes and living as appreciated members of our families, dogs do not think or learn exactly the same way people do. Even if you love your dog like a child, you must remember to respect the fact that he is actually a dog.

Dogs have no idea when their behavior is inappropriate from a human perspective. They are not aware of the value of possessions they chew or of messes they make or the worry they sometimes seem to cause. While people tend to look at behavior as good and bad or right and wrong, dogs just discover what works and what doesn't work. Then they behave accordingly, learning from their own experiences and increasing or reducing behaviors to improve results for themselves.

You might wonder, "But don't dogs want to please us"? My answer is yes, provided your pleasure reflects back to them in positive ways they can feel and appreciate. Dogs do things for *dog* reasons, and everything they do works for them in some way or they wouldn't be doing it!

The Social Dog

Our pets descended from animals who lived in tightly knit, cooperative social groups. Though far removed in appearance and lifestyle from their ancestors, our dogs still relate in many of the same ways their wild relatives did. And in their relationships with one another, wild canids either lead or follow.

Canine ranking relationships are not about cruelty and power; they are about achievement and abilities. Competent dogs with high levels of drive and confidence step up, while deferring dogs step aside. But followers don't get the short end of the stick; they benefit from the security of having a more competent dog at the helm.

Our domestic dogs still measure themselves against other members of their group—us! Dog owners whose actions lead to positive results have willing, secure followers. But dogs may step up and fill the void or cut loose and do their own thing when their people fail to show capable leadership. When dogs are pushy, aggressive, and rude, or independent and unwilling, it's not because they have designs on the role of "master." It is more likely their owners failed to provide consistent leadership.

Dogs in training benefit from their handler's good leadership. Their education flows smoothly because they are impressed. Being in charge doesn't require you to physically dominate or punish your dog. You simply need to make some subtle changes in the way you relate to him every day.

Lead Your Pack!

Create schedules and structure daily activities. Dogs are creatures of habit and routines will create security. Feed meals at the same times each day and also try to schedule regular walks, training practices, and toilet outings. Your predictability will help your dog be patient.

Ask your dog to perform a task. Before releasing him to food or freedom, have him do something as simple as sit on command. Teach him that cooperation earns great results!

Give a release prompt (such as "let's go") when going through doors leading outside. This is a better idea than allowing your impatient pup to rush past you.

Pet your dog when he is calm, not when he is excited. Turn your touch into a tool that relaxes and settles.

Reward desirable rather than inappropriate behavior. Petting a jumping dog (who hasn't been invited up) reinforces jumping. Pet sitting dogs, and only invite lap dogs up after they've first "asked" by waiting for your invitation.

Replace personal punishment with positive reinforcement. Show a dog what *to do,* and motivate him to want to do it, and there will be no need to punish him for what he should *not do.* Dogs naturally follow, without the need for force or harshness.

Play creatively and appropriately. Your dog will learn the most about his social rank when he is playing with you. During play, dogs work to control toys and try to get the best of one another in a friendly way. The wrong sorts of play can create problems: For example, tug of war can lead to aggressiveness. Allowing your dog to control toys during play may result in possessive guarding when he has something he really values, such as a bone. Dogs who are chased during play may later run away from you when you approach to leash them. The right kinds of play will help increase your dog's social confidence while you gently assert your leadership.

How Dogs Learn (and How They Don't)

Dog training begins as a meeting of minds—yours and your dog's. Though the end goal may be to get your dog's body to behave in a specific way, training starts as a mind game. Your dog is learning all the time by observing the consequences of his actions and social interactions. He is always seeking out what he perceives as desirable and trying to avoid what he perceives as undesirable.

He will naturally repeat a behavior that either brings him more good stuff or makes bad stuff go away (these are both types of reinforcement). He will naturally avoid a behavior that brings him more bad stuff or makes the good stuff go away (these are both types of punishment).

Both reinforcement and punishment can be perceived as either the direct result of something the dog did himself, or as coming from an outside source.

Using Life's Rewards

Your best friend is smart and he is also cooperative. When the best things in life can only be had by working with you, your dog will view you as a facilitator. You unlock doors to all of the positively reinforcing experiences he values: his freedom, his friends at the park, food, affection, walks, and play. The trained dog accompanies you through those doors and waits to see what working with you will bring.

Rewarding your dog for good behavior is called positive reinforcement, and, as we've just seen, it increases the likelihood that he will repeat that behavior. The perfect reward is anything your dog wants that is safe and appropriate. Don't limit yourself to toys, treats, and things that come directly from you. Harness life's positives—barking at squirrels, chasing a falling leaf, bounding away from you at the dog park, pausing for a moment to sniff everything—and allow your dog to earn access to those things as rewards that come from cooperating with you. When he looks at you, when he sits, when he comes when you call—any prompted behavior can earn one of life's rewards. When he works with you, he earns the things he most appreciates; but when he tries to get those things on his own, he cannot. Rather than seeing you as someone who always says "no," your dog will view you as the one who says "let's go!" He will *want* to follow.

What About Punishment?

Not only is it unnecessary to personally punish dogs, it is abusive. No matter how convinced you are that your dog "knows right from wrong," in reality he will associate personal punishment with the punisher. The resulting cowering, "guilty"-looking postures are actually displays of submission and fear. Later, when the punisher isn't around and the coast is clear, the same behavior he was punished for—such as raiding a trash can—might bring a self-delivered, very tasty result. The punished dog hasn't learned not to misbehave; he has learned to not get caught.

Purely Positive Reinforcement

With positive training, we emphasize teaching dogs what they should do to earn reinforcements, rather than punishing them for unwanted behaviors.

- Focus on teaching "do" rather than "don't." For example, a sitting dog isn't jumping.
- Use positive reinforcers that are valuable to your dog and the situation: A tired dog values rest; a confined dog values freedom.
- Play (appropriately)!
- Be a consistent leader.
- Set your dog up for success by anticipating and preventing problems.
- Notice and reward desirable behavior, and give him lots of attention when he is being good.
- Train ethically. Use humane methods and equipment that do not frighten or hurt your dog.
- When you are angry, walk away and plan a positive strategy.
- Keep practice sessions short and sweet. Five to ten minutes, three to five times a day is best.

Does punishment ever have a place in dog training? Many people will heartily insist it does not. But dog owners often get frustrated as they try to stick to the path of all-positive reinforcement. It sure sounds great, but is it realistic, or even natural, to *never* say "no" to your dog?

A wild dog's life is not *all* positive. Hunger and thirst are both examples of negative reinforcement; the resulting discomfort motivates the wild dog to seek food and water. He encounters natural aversives such as pesky insects; mats in his coat; cold days; rainy days; sweltering hot days; and occasional run-ins with thorns, brambles, skunks, bees, and other nastiness. These all affect his behavior, as he tries to avoid the bad stuff whenever possible. The wild dog also occasionally encounters social punishers from others in his group when he gets too pushy. Starting with a growl or a snap from Mom, and later some mild and ritualized discipline from other members of his four-legged family, he learns to modify behaviors that elicit grouchy responses.

Our pet dogs don't naturally experience all positive results either, because they learn from their surroundings and from social experiences with other dogs. Watch a group of pet dogs playing together and you'll see a very old educational system still being used. As they wrestle and attempt to assert themselves, you'll notice many mouth-on-neck moments. Their playful biting is inhibited, with no intention to cause harm, but their message is clear: "Say uncle or this could hurt more!"

Observing that punishment does occur in nature, some people may feel compelled to try to be like the big wolf with their pet dogs. Becoming aggressive or heavy-handed with your pet will backfire! Your dog will not be impressed, nor will he want to follow you. Punishment causes dogs to change their behavior to avoid or escape discomfort and threats. Threatened dogs will either become very passive and offer submissive, appeasing postures, attempt to flee, or rise to the occasion and fight back. When people personally punish their dogs in an angry manner, one of these three defensive mechanisms will be triggered. Which one depends on a dog's genetic temperament as well as his past social experiences. Since we don't want to make our pets feel the need to avoid or escape us, personal punishment has no place in our training.

Remote Consequences

Sometimes, however, all-positive reinforcement is just not enough. That's because not all reinforcement comes from us. An inappropriate behavior can be self-reinforcing—just doing it makes the dog feel better in some way, whether you are there to say "good boy!" or not. Some examples are eating garbage, pulling the stuffing out of your sofa, barking at passersby, or urinating on the floor.

Although you don't want to personally punish your dog, the occasional deterrent may be called for to help derail these kinds of self-rewarding misbehaviors. In these cases, mild forms of impersonal or remote punishment can be used as part of a correction. The goal isn't to make your dog feel bad or to "know he has done wrong," but to help redirect him to alternate behaviors that are more acceptable to you.

You do this by pairing a slightly startling, totally impersonal sound with an equally impersonal and *very mild* remote consequence. The impersonal sound might be a single shake of an empty plastic pop bottle with pennies in it, held out of your dog's sight. Or you could use a vocal expression such as "eh!" delivered with you looking *away* from your misbehaving dog.

The Problems with Personal Punishment

- Personally punished dogs are not taught appropriate behaviors.
- Personally punished dogs only stop misbehaving when they are caught or interrupted, but they don't learn not to misbehave when they are alone.
- Personally punished dogs become shy, fearful, and distrusting.
- Personally punished dogs may become defensively aggressive.
- Personally punished dogs become suppressed and inhibited.
- Personally punished dogs become stressed, triggering stress-reducing behaviors that their owners interpret as acts of spite, triggering even more punishment.
- Personally punished dogs have stressed owners.
- Personally punished dogs may begin to repeat behaviors they have been taught will result in negative, but predictable, attention.
- Personally punished dogs are more likely to be given away than are positively trained dogs.

Pair your chosen sound—the penny bottle or "eh!"—with either a slight tug on his collar or a sneaky spritz on the rump from a water bottle. Do this right *as* he touches something he should not; bad timing will confuse your dog and undermine your training success.

To keep things under your control and make sure you get the timing right, it's best to do this as a setup. "Accidentally" drop a shoe on the floor, and then help your dog learn some things are best avoided. As he sniffs the shoe say "eh!" without looking at him and give a *slight* tug against his collar. This sound will quickly become meaningful as a correction all by itself—sometimes after just one setup—making the tug correction obsolete. The tug lets your dog see that you were right; going for that shoe *was* a bad idea! Your wise dog will be more likely to heed your warning next time, and probably move closer to you where it's safe. Be a good friend and pick up the nasty shoe. He'll be relieved and you'll look heroic. Later, when he's home alone and encounters a stray shoe, he'll want to give it a wide berth.

Your negative marking sound will come in handy in the future, when your dog begins to venture down the wrong behavioral path. The goal is not to announce your disapproval or to threaten your dog. You are not telling him to stop or showing how *you* feel about his behavior. You are sounding a warning to a friend who's venturing off toward danger—"I wouldn't if I were you!" Suddenly, there is an abrupt, rather startling, noise! Now is the moment to redirect him and help him earn positive reinforcement. That interrupted behavior will become something he wants to avoid in the future, but he won't want to avoid you.

Practical Commands for Family Pets

Before you begin training your dog, let's look at some equipment you'll want to have on hand:

- **A buckle collar** is fine for most dogs. If your dog pulls *very* hard, try a head collar, a device similar to a horse halter that helps reduce pulling by turning the dog's head. *Do not* use a choke chain (sometimes called a training collar), because they cause physical harm even when used correctly.
- **Six-foot training leash and twenty-six–foot retractable leash.**
- **A few empty plastic soda bottles with about twenty pennies in each one.** This will be used to impersonally interrupt misbehaviors before redirecting dogs to more positive activities.
- **A favorite squeaky toy,** to motivate, attract attention, and reward your dog during training.

Baby Steps

Allow your young pup to drag a short, lightweight leash attached to a buckle collar for a few *supervised* moments, several times each day. At first the leash may annoy him and he may jump around a bit trying to get away from it. Distract him with your squeaky toy or a bit of his kibble and he'll quickly get used to his new "tail."

Begin walking him on the leash by holding the end and following him. As he adapts, you can begin to assert gentle direct pressure to teach him to follow you.

Lure your dog to take just a few steps with you on the leash by being inviting and enthusiastic. Make sure you reward him for his efforts.

Don't jerk or yank, or he will become afraid to walk when the leash is on. If he becomes hesitant, squat down facing him and let him figure out that by moving toward you he is safe and secure. If he remains confused or frightened and doesn't come to you, go to him and help him understand that you provide safe harbor while he's on the leash. Then back away a few steps and try again to lure him to you. As he learns that you are the "home base," he'll want to follow when you walk a few steps, waiting for you to stop, squat down, and make him feel great.

So Attached to You!

The next step in training your dog—and this is a very important one—is to begin spending at least an hour or more each day with him on a four- to six-foot leash,

Tethering your dog is great way to keep him calm and under control, but still with you.

held by or tethered to you. This training will increase his attachment to you—literally!—as you sit quietly or walk about, tending to your household business. When you are quiet, he'll learn it is time to settle; when you are active, he'll learn to move with you. Tethering also keeps him out of trouble when you are busy but still want his company. It is a great alternative to confining a dog, and can be used instead of crating any time you're home and need to slow him down a bit.

Rotating your dog from supervised freedom to tethered time to some quiet time in the crate or his gated area gives him a diverse and balanced day while he is learning. Two confined or tethered hours is the most you should require of your dog in one stretch, before changing to some supervised freedom, play, or a walk.

The dog in training may, at times, be stressed by all of the changes he is dealing with. Provide a stress outlet, such as a toy to chew on, when he is confined or tethered. He will settle into his quiet time more quickly and completely. Always be sure to provide several rounds of daily play and free time (in a fenced area or on your retractable leash) in addition to plenty of chewing materials.

Dog Talk

Dogs don't speak in words, but they do have a language—body language. They use postures, vocalizations, movements, facial gestures, odors, and touch—usually with their mouths—to communicate what they are feeling and thinking.

We also "speak" using body language. We have quite an array of postures, movements, and facial gestures that accompany our touch and language as we attempt to communicate with our pets. And our dogs can quickly figure us out!

Alone, without associations, words are just noises. But, because we pair them with meaningful body language, our dogs make the connection. Dogs can really learn to understand much of what we *say*, if what we *do* at the same time is consistent.

The Positive Marker

Start your dog's education with one of the best tricks in dog training: Pair various positive reinforcers—food, a toy, touch—with a sound such as a click on a clicker (which you can get at the pet supply store) or a spoken word like "good!" or "yes!" This will enable you to later "mark" your dog's desirable behaviors.

It seems too easy: Just say "yes!" and give the dog his toy. (Or use whatever sound and reward you have chosen.) Later, when you make your marking sound right at the instant your dog does the right thing, he will know you are going to be giving him something good for that particular action. And he'll be eager to repeat the behavior to hear you mark it again!

Next, you must teach your dog to understand the meaning of cues you'll be using to ask him to perform specific behaviors. This is easy, too. Does he already do things you might like him to do on command? Of course! He lies down, he sits, he picks things up, he drops them again, he comes to you. All of the behaviors you'd like to control are already part of your dog's natural repertoire. The trick is getting him to offer those behaviors when you ask for them. And that means you have to teach him to associate a particular behavior on his part with a particular behavior on your part.

Sit Happens

Teach your dog an important new rule: From now on, he is only touched and petted when he is either sitting or lying down. You won't need to ask him to sit; in fact, you should not. Just keeping him tethered near you so there isn't much to do but stand, be ignored, or settle, and wait until sit happens.

He may pester you a bit, but be stoic and unresponsive. Starting now, when *you* are sitting down, a sitting dog is the only one you see and pay attention to. He will eventually sit, and as he does, attach the word "sit"—but don't be too excited or he'll jump right back up. Now mark with your positive sound that promises something good, then reward him with a slow, quiet, settling pet.

Training requires consistent reinforcement. Ask others to also wait until your dog is sitting and calm to touch him, and he will associate being petted with being relaxed. Be sure you train your dog to associate everyone's touch with quiet bonding.

Reinforcing "Sit" as a Command

Since your dog now understands one concept of working for a living—sit to earn petting—you can begin to shape and reinforce his desire to sit. Hold toys, treats, his bowl of food, and turn into a statue. But don't prompt him to sit! Instead, remain frozen and unavailable, looking somewhere out into space, over his head. He will put on a bit of a show, trying to get a response from you, and may offer various behaviors, but only one will push your button—sitting. Wait for him to offer the "right" behavior, and when he does, you unfreeze. Say "sit," then mark with an excited "good!" and give him the toy or treat with a release command—"OK!"

When you notice spontaneous sits occurring, be sure to take advantage of those free opportunities to make your command sequence meaningful and positive. Say "sit" as you observe sit happen—then mark with "good!" and praise, pet, or reward the dog. Soon, every time you look at your dog he'll be sitting and looking right back at you!

Now, after thirty days of purely positive practice, it's time to give him a test. When he is just walking around doing his own thing, suddenly ask him to sit. He'll probably do it right away. If he doesn't, do *not* repeat your command, or you'll just undermine its meaning ("sit" means sit *now;* the command is not "sit, sit, sit, sit"). Instead, get something he likes and let him know you have it. Wait for him to offer the sit—he will—then say "sit!" and complete your marking and rewarding sequence.

OK

"OK" will probably rate as one of your dog's favorite words. It's like the word "recess" to schoolchildren. It is the word used to release your dog from a command.

You can introduce "OK" during your "sit" practice. When he gets up from a sit, say "OK" to tell him the sitting is finished. Soon that sound will mean "freedom."

Make it even more meaningful and positive. Whenever he spontaneously bounds away, say "OK!" Squeak a toy, and when he notices and shows interest, toss it for him.

Down

I've mentioned that you should only pet your dog when he is either sitting or lying down. Now, using the approach I've just introduced for "sit," teach your dog to lie down. You will be a statue, and hold something he would like to get but that you'll only release to a dog who is lying down. It helps to lower the desired item to the floor in front of him, still not speaking and not letting him have it until he offers you the new behavior you are seeking.

He may offer a sit and then wait expectantly, but you must make him keep searching for the new trick that triggers your generosity. Allow your dog to experiment and find the right answer, even if he has to search around for it first. When he lands on "down" and learns it is another behavior that works, he'll offer it more quickly the next time.

Don't say "down" until he lies down, to tightly associate your prompt with the correct behavior. To say "down, down, down" as he is sitting, looking at you, or pawing at the toy would make "down" mean those behaviors instead! Whichever behavior he offers, a training opportunity has been created. Once you've attached

Lower your dog's reward to the floor to help him figure out what behavior will earn him his reward.

and shaped both sitting and lying down, you can ask for both behaviors with your verbal prompts, "sit" or "down." Be sure to only reinforce the "correct" reply!

Stay

"Stay" can easily be taught as an extension of what you've already been practicing. To teach "stay," you follow the entire sequence for reinforcing a "sit" or "down," except you wait a bit longer before you give the release word, "OK!" Wait a second or two longer during each practice before saying "OK!" and releasing your dog to the positive reinforcer (toy, treat, or one of life's other rewards).

If he gets up before you've said "OK," you have two choices: pretend the release was your idea and quickly interject "OK!" as he breaks; or, if he is more experienced and practiced, mark the behavior with your correction sound— "eh!"— and then gently put him back on the spot, wait for him to lie down, and begin again. Be sure the next three practices are a success. Ask him to wait for just a second, and release him before he can be wrong. You need to keep your dog feeling like more of a success than a failure as you begin to test his training in increasingly more distracting and difficult situations.

As he gets the hang of it—he stays until you say "OK"— you can gradually push for longer times—up to a minute on a sit-stay, and up to three minutes on

You can step on the leash to help your dog understand the down-stay, but only do this when he is already lying down. You don't want to hurt him!

a down-stay. You can also gradually add distractions and work in new environments. To add a minor self-correction for the down-stay, stand on the dog's leash after he lies down, allowing about three inches of slack. If tries to get up before you've said "OK," he'll discover it doesn't work.

Do not step on the leash to make your dog lie down! This could badly hurt his neck, and will destroy his trust in you. Remember, we are teaching our dogs to make the best choices, not inflicting our answers upon them!

Come

Rather than thinking of "come" as an action—"come to me"—think of it as a place—"the dog is sitting in front of me, facing me." Since your dog by now really likes sitting to earn your touch and other positive reinforcement, he's likely to sometimes sit directly in front of you, facing you, all on his own. When this happens, give it a specific name: "come."

Now follow the rest of the training steps you have learned to make him like doing it and reinforce the behavior by practicing it any chance you get. Anything your dog wants and likes could be earned as a result of his first offering the sit-in-front known as "come."

You can help guide him into the right location. Use your hands as "landing gear" and pat the insides of your legs at his nose level. Do this while backing up a bit, to help him maneuver to the straight-in-front, facing-you position. Don't say the word "come" while he's maneuvering, because he hasn't! You are trying to make "come" the end result, not the work in progress.

You can also help your dog by marking his movement in the right direction: Use your positive sound or word to promise he is getting warm. When he finally sits facing you, enthusiastically say "come," mark again with your positive word, and release him with an enthusiastic "OK!" Make it so worth his while, with lots of play and praise, that he can't wait for you to ask him to come again!

Building a Better Recall

Practice, practice, practice. Now, practice some more. Teach your dog that all good things in life hinge upon him first sitting in front of you

Pat the insides of your legs to show your dog exactly where you like him to sit when you say "come."

in a behavior named "come." When you think he really has got it, test him by asking him to "come" as you gradually add distractions and change locations. Expect setbacks as you make these changes and practice accordingly. Lower your expectations and make his task easier so he is able to get it right. Use those distractions as rewards, when they are appropriate. For example, let him check out the interesting leaf that blew by as a reward for first coming to you and ignoring it.

Add distance and call your dog to come while he is on his retractable leash. If he refuses and sits looking at you blankly, *do not* jerk, tug, "pop," or reel him in. Do nothing! It is his move; wait to see what behavior he offers. He'll either begin to approach (mark the behavior with an excited "good!"), sit and do nothing (just keep waiting), or he'll try to move in some direction other than toward you. If he tries to leave, use your correction marker—"eh!"— and bring him to a stop by letting him walk to the end of the leash, *not* by jerking him. Now walk to him in a neutral manner, and don't jerk or show any disapproval. Gently bring him back to the spot where he was when you called him, then back away and face him, still waiting and not reissuing your command. Let him keep examining his options until he finds the one that works—yours!

If you have practiced everything I've suggested so far and given your dog a chance to really learn what "come" means, he is well aware of what you want and is quite intelligently weighing all his options. The only way he'll know your way is the one that works is to be allowed to examine his other choices and discover that they *don't* work.

Sooner or later every dog tests his training. Don't be offended or angry when your dog tests you. No matter how positive you've made it, he won't always want to do everything you ask, every time. When he explores the "what happens if I don't" scenario, your training is being strengthened. He will discover through his own process of trial and error that the best—and only—way out of a command he really doesn't feel compelled to obey is to obey it.

Let's Go

Many pet owners wonder if they can retain control while walking their dogs and still allow at least some running in front, sniffing, and playing. You might worry that allowing your dog occasional freedom could result in him expecting it all the time, leading to a testy, leash-straining walk. It's possible for both parties on the leash to have an enjoyable experience by implementing and reinforcing well-thought-out training techniques.

Begin by making word associations you'll use on your walks. Give the dog some slack on the leash, and as he starts to walk away from you say "OK" and begin to follow him.

Do not let him drag you; set the pace even when he is being given a turn at being the leader. Whenever he starts to pull, just come to a standstill and refuse to move (or refuse to allow him to continue forward) until there is slack in the leash. Do this correction without saying anything at all. When he isn't pulling, you may decide to just stand still and let him sniff about within the range the slack leash allows, or you may even mosey along following him. After a few minutes of "recess," it is time to work. Say something like "that's it" or "time's up," close the distance between you and your dog, and touch him.

Next say "let's go" (or whatever command you want to use to mean "follow me as we walk"). Turn and walk off, and, if he follows, mark his behavior with "good!" Then stop, squat down, and let him catch you. Make him glad he did! Start again,

Give your dog slack on his leash as you walk and let him make the decision to walk with you.

and do a few transitions as he gets the hang of your follow-the-leader game, speeding up, slowing down, and trying to make it fun. When you stop, he gets to catch up and receive some deserved positive reinforcement. Don't forget that's the reason he is following you, so be sure to make it worth his while!

Require him to remain attentive to you. Do not allow sniffing, playing, eliminating, or pulling during your time as leader on a walk. If he seems to get distracted—which, by the way, is the main reason dogs walk poorly with their people— change direction or pace without saying a word. Just help him realize "oops, I lost track of my human." Do not jerk his neck and say "heel"—this will make the word "heel" mean pain in the neck and will not encourage him to cooperate with you. Don't repeat "let's go," either. He needs to figure out that it is his job to keep track of and follow

When your dog catches up with you, make sure you let him know what a great dog he is!

you if he wants to earn the positive benefits you provide.

The best reward you can give a dog for performing an attentive, controlled walk is a few minutes of walking without all of the controls. Of course, he must remain on a leash even during the "recess" parts of the walk, but allowing him to discriminate between attentive following—"let's go"—and having a few moments of relaxation—"OK"—will increase his willingness to work.

Intersperse periods of attentive walking, where your dog is on a shorter leash, with periods on a slack leash, where he is allowed to look and sniff around.

Training for Attention

Your dog pretty much has a one-track mind. Once he is focused on something, everything else is excluded. This can be great, for instance, when he's focusing on you! But it can also be dangerous if, for example, his attention is riveted on the bunny he is chasing and he does not hear you call—that is, not unless he has been trained to pay attention when you say his name.

When you call your dog's name, you will again be seeking a specific response—eye contact. The best way to teach this is to trigger his alerting response by making a noise with your mouth, such as whistling or a kissing sound, and then immediately doing something he'll find very intriguing.

You can play a treasure hunt game to help teach him to regard his name as a request for attention. As a bonus, you can reinforce the rest of his new vocabulary at the same time.

Treasure Hunt

Make a kissing sound, then jump up and find a dog toy or dramatically raid the fridge and rather noisily eat a piece of cheese. After doing this twice, make a kissing sound and then look at your dog.

Of course he is looking at you! He is waiting to see if that sound—the kissing sound—means you're going to go hunting again. After all, you're so good at it!

When you say your dog's name, you'll want him to make eye contact with you. Begin teaching this by making yourself so intriguing that he can't help but look.

Because he is looking, say his name, mark with "good," then go hunting and find his toy. Release it to him with an "OK." At any point if he follows you, attach your "let's go!" command; if he leaves you, give permission with "OK."

Using this approach, he cannot be wrong—any behavior your dog offers can be named. You can add things like "take it" when he picks up a toy, and "thank you" when he happens to drop one. Many opportunities to make your new vocabulary meaningful and positive can be found within this simple training game.

Problems to watch out for when teaching the treasure hunt:

- You really do not want your dog to come to you when you call his name (later, when you try to engage his attention to ask him to stay, he'll already be on his way toward you). You just want him to look at you.
- Saying "watch me, watch me" doesn't teach your dog to *offer* his attention. It just makes you a background noise.
- Don't lure your dog's attention with the reward. Get his attention and then reward him for looking. Try holding a toy in one hand with your arm stretched out to your side. Wait until he looks at you rather than the toy. Now say his name then mark with "good!" and release the toy. As he goes for it, say "OK."

To get your dog's attention, try holding his toy with your arm out to your side. Wait until he looks at you, then mark the moment and give him the toy.

Teaching Cooperation

Never punish your dog for failing to obey you or try to punish him into compliance. Bribing, repeating yourself, and doing a behavior for him all avoid the real issue of dog training—his will. He must be helped to be willing, not made to achieve tasks. Good dog training helps your dog want to obey. He learns that he can gain what he values most through cooperation and compliance, and can't gain those things any other way.

Your dog is learning to *earn,* rather than expect, the good things in life. And you've become much more important to him than you were before. Because you are allowing him to experiment and learn, he doesn't have to be forced, manipulated, or bribed. When he wants something, he can gain it by cooperating with you. One of those "somethings"—and a great reward you shouldn't underestimate—is your positive attention, paid to him with love and sincere approval!

Chapter 10

House-training Your Beagle

Excerpted from Housetraining: An Owner's Guide to a Happy Healthy Pet, 1st Edition, by September Morn

By the time puppies are about 3 weeks old, they start to follow their mother around. When they are a few steps away from their clean sleeping area, the mama dog stops. The pups try to nurse but mom won't allow it. The pups mill around in frustration, then nature calls and they all urinate and defecate here, away from their bed. The mother dog returns to the nest, with her brood waddling behind her. Their first housetraining lesson has been a success.

The next one to housetrain puppies should be their breeder. The breeder watches as the puppies eliminate, then deftly removes the soiled papers and replaces them with clean papers before the pups can traipse back through their messes. He has wisely arranged the puppies' space so their bed, food, and drinking water are as far away from the elimination area as possible. This way, when the pups follow their mama, they will move away from their sleeping and eating area before eliminating. This habit will help the pups be easily housetrained.

Your Housetraining Shopping List

While your puppy's mother and breeder are getting her started on good housetraining habits, you'll need to do some shopping. If you have all the essentials in place before your dog arrives, it will be easier to help her learn the rules from day one.

Newspaper: The younger your puppy and larger her breed, the more newspapers you'll need. Newspaper is absorbent, abundant, cheap, and convenient.

Puddle Pads: If you prefer not to stockpile newspaper, a commercial alternative is puddle pads. These thick paper pads can be purchased under several trade names at pet supply stores. The pads have waterproof backing, so puppy urine doesn't seep through onto the floor. Their disadvantages are that they will cost you more than newspapers and that they contain plastics that are not biodegradable.

Poop Removal Tool: There are several types of poop removal tools available. Some are designed with a separate pan and rake, and others have the handles hinged like scissors. Some scoops need two hands for operation, while others are designed for one-handed use. Try out the different brands at your pet supply store. Put a handful of pebbles or dog kibble on the floor and then pick them up with each type of scoop to determine which works best for you.

Plastic Bags: When you take your dog outside your yard, you *must* pick up after her. Dog waste is unsightly, smelly, and can harbor disease. In many cities and towns, the law mandates dog owners clean up pet waste deposited on public ground. Picking up after your dog using a plastic bag scoop is simple. Just put your hand inside the bag, like a mitten, and then grab the droppings. Turn the bag inside out, tie the top, and that's that.

Crate: To housetrain a puppy, you will need some way to confine her when you're unable to supervise. A dog crate is a secure way to confine your dog for short periods during the day and to use as a comfortable bed at night. Crates come in wire mesh and in plastic. The wire ones are foldable to store flat in a smaller space. The plastic ones are more cozy, draft-free, and quiet, and are approved for airline travel.

Baby Gates: Since you shouldn't crate a dog for more than an hour or two at a time during the day, baby gates are a good way to limit your dog's freedom in the house. Be sure the baby gates you use are safe. The old-fashioned wooden, expanding lattice type has seriously injured a number of children by collapsing and trapping a leg, arm, or neck. That type of gate can hurt a puppy, too, so use the modern grid type gates instead. You'll need more than one baby gate if you have several doorways to close off.

Exercise Pen: Portable exercise pens are great when you have a young pup or a small dog. These metal or plastic pens are made of rectangular panels that are hinged together. The pens are freestanding, sturdy, foldable, and can be carried like a suitcase. You could set one up in your kitchen as the pup's daytime corral, and then take it outdoors to contain your pup while you garden or just sit and enjoy the day.

Enzymatic Cleaner: All dogs make housetraining mistakes. Accept this and be ready for it by buying an enzymatic cleaner made especially for pet accidents. Dogs like to eliminate where they have done it before, and lingering smells lead them to those spots. Ordinary household cleaners may remove all the odors you can smell, but only an enzymatic cleaner will remove everything your dog can smell.

The First Day

Housetraining is a matter of establishing good habits in your dog. That means you never want her to learn anything she will eventually have to unlearn. Start off housetraining on the right foot by teaching your dog that you prefer her to eliminate outside. Designate a potty area in your backyard (if you have one) or in the street in front of your home and take your dog to it as soon as you arrive home. Let her sniff a bit and, when she squats to go, give the action a name: "potty" or "do it" or anything else you won't be embarrassed to say in public. Eventually your dog will associate that word with the act and will eliminate on command. When she's finished, praise her with "good potty!"

That first day, take your puppy out to the potty area frequently. Although she may not eliminate every time, you are establishing a routine: You take her to her spot, ask her to eliminate, and praise her when she does.

Take your pup out frequently to her special potty spot and praise her when she goes.

Don't Overuse the Crate

A crate serves well as a dog's overnight bed, but you should not leave the dog in her crate for more than an hour or two during the day. Throughout the day, she needs to play and exercise. She is likely to want to drink some water and will undoubtedly eliminate. Confining your dog all day will give her no option but to soil her crate. This is not just unpleasant for you and the dog, but it reinforces bad cleanliness habits. And crating a pup for the whole day is abusive. Don't do it.

Just before bedtime, take your dog to her potty area once more. Stand by and wait until she produces. Do not put your dog to bed for the night until she has eliminated. Be patient and calm. This is not the time to play with or excite your dog. If she's too excited, a pup not only won't eliminate, she probably won't want to sleep either.

Most dogs, even young ones, will not soil their beds if they can avoid it. For this reason, a sleeping crate can be a tremendous help during housetraining. Being crated at night can help a dog develop the muscles that control elimination. So after your dog has emptied out, put her to bed in her crate.

A good place to put your dog's sleeping crate is near your own bed. Dogs are pack animals, so they feel safer sleeping with others in a common area. In your bedroom, the pup will be near you and you'll be close enough to hear when she wakes during the night and needs to eliminate.

Little puppies can't hold their urine in all night. Take your pup out when she needs to go, even if it's the middle of the night.

Pups under 4 months old often are not able to hold their urine all night. If your puppy has settled down to sleep but awakens and fusses a few hours later, she probably needs to go out. For the best housetraining progress, take your pup to her elimination area whenever she needs to go, even in the wee hours of the morning.

Your pup may soil in her crate if you ignore her late night urgency. It's unfair to let this happen, and it sends the wrong message about your expectations for cleanliness. Resign yourself to this midnight outing and just get up and take the pup out. Your pup will outgrow this need soon and will learn in the process that she can count on you, and you'll wake happily each morning to a clean dog.

The next morning, the very first order of business is to take your pup out to eliminate. Don't forget to take her to her special potty spot, ask her to eliminate, and then praise her when she does. After your pup empties out in the morning, give her breakfast, and then take her to her potty area again. After that, she shouldn't need to eliminate again right away, so you can allow her some free playtime. Keep an eye on the pup though, because when she pauses in play she may need to go potty. Take her to the right spot, give the command, and praise if she produces.

Confine Your Pup

A pup or dog who has not finished housetraining should *never* be allowed the run of the house unattended. A new dog (especially a puppy) with unlimited access to your house will make her own choices about where to eliminate. Vigilance during your new dog's first few weeks in your home will pay big dividends. Every potty mistake delays housetraining progress; every success speeds it along.

Prevent problems by setting up a controlled environment for your new pet. A good place for a puppy corral is often the kitchen. Kitchens almost always have waterproof or easily cleaned floors, which is a distinct asset with leaky pups. A bathroom, laundry room, or enclosed porch could be used for a puppy corral, but the kitchen is generally the best location. Kitchens are a meeting place and a hub of activity for many

> **TIP**
>
> **Water**
>
> Make sure your dog has access to clean water at all times. Limiting the amount of water a dog drinks is not necessary for housetraining success and can be very dangerous. A dog needs water to digest food, to maintain a proper body temperature and proper blood volume, and to clean her system of toxins and wastes. A healthy dog will automatically drink the right amount. Do not restrict water intake. Controlling your dog's access to water is not the key to housetraining her; controlling her access to everything else in your home is.

Keep your puppy in a confined area, so she has no chance to make mistakes. Set her up for success.

families, and a puppy will learn better manners when she is socialized thoroughly with family, friends, and nice strangers.

The way you structure your pup's corral area is very important. Her bed, food, and water should be at the opposite end of the corral from the potty area. When you first get your pup, spread newspaper over the rest of the floor of her playpen corral. Lay the papers at least four pages thick and be sure to overlap the edges. As you note the pup's progress, you can remove the papers nearest the sleeping and eating corner. Gradually decrease the size of the papered area until only the end where you want the pup to eliminate is covered. If you will be training your dog to eliminate outside, place newspaper at the end of the corral that is closest to the door that leads outdoors. That way as she moves away from the clean area to the papered area, the pup will also form the habit of heading toward the door to go out.

Maintain a scent marker for the pup's potty area by reserving a small soiled piece of paper when you clean up. Place this piece, with her scent of urine, under the top sheet of the clean papers you spread. This will cue your pup where to eliminate.

Most dog owners use a combination of indoor papers and outdoor elimination areas. When the pup is left by herself in the corral, she can potty on the ever-present newspaper. When you are available to take the pup outside, she can do her business in the outdoor spot. It is not difficult to switch a pup from indoor paper training to outdoor elimination. Owners of large pups often switch early, but potty papers are still useful if the pup spends time in her indoor corral while you're away. Use the papers as long as your pup needs them. If you come home and they haven't been soiled, you are ahead.

When setting up your pup's outdoor yard, put the lounging area as far away as possible from the potty area, just as with the indoor corral setup. People with large yards, for example, might leave a patch unmowed at the edge of the lawn to serve as the dog's elimination area. Other dog owners teach the dog to relieve herself in a designated corner of a deck or patio. For an apartment-dwelling city dog, the outdoor potty area might be a tiny balcony or the curb. Each dog owner has somewhat different expectations for their dog. Teach your dog to eliminate in a spot that suits your environment and lifestyle.

Be sure to pick up droppings in your yard at least once a day. Dogs have a natural desire to stay far away from their own excrement, and if too many piles litter the ground, your dog won't want to walk through it and will start eliminating elsewhere. Leave just one small piece of feces in the potty area to remind your dog where the right spot is located.

To help a pup adapt to the change from indoors to outdoors, take one of her potty papers outside to the new elimination area. Let the pup stand on the paper when she goes potty outdoors. Each day for four days, reduce the size of the paper by half. By the fifth day, the pup, having used a smaller and smaller piece of paper to stand on, will probably just go to that spot and eliminate.

Take your pup to her outdoor potty place frequently throughout the day. A puppy can hold her urine for only about as many hours as her age in months, and will move her bowels as many times a day as she eats. So a 2-month-old pup will urinate about every two hours, while at 4 months she can manage about four hours between piddles. Pups vary somewhat in their rate of development, so this is not a hard and fast rule. It does, however, present a realistic idea of how long a pup can be left without access to a potty place. Past 4 months, her potty trips will be less frequent.

When you take the dog outdoors to her spot, keep her leashed so that she won't wander away. Stand quietly and let her sniff around in the designated area. If your pup starts to leave before she has eliminated, gently lead her back and remind her to go. If your pup sniffs at the spot, praise her calmly, say the command word, and just wait. If she produces, praise serenely, then give her time to sniff around a little more. She may not be finished, so give her time to go again before allowing her to play and explore her new home.

If you find yourself waiting more than five minutes for your dog to potty, take her back inside. Watch your pup carefully for twenty minutes, not giving her any opportunity to slip away to eliminate unnoticed. If you are too busy to watch the pup, put her in her crate. After twenty minutes, take her to the

Take your dog out frequently for regularly scheduled walks.

outdoor potty spot again and tell her what to do. If you're unsuccessful after five minutes, crate the dog again. Give her another chance to eliminate in fifteen or twenty minutes. Eventually, she will have to go.

Watch Your Pup

Be vigilant and don't let the pup make a mistake in the house. Each time you successfully anticipate elimination and take your pup to the potty spot, you'll move a step closer to your goal. Stay aware of your puppy's needs. If you ignore the pup, she will make mistakes and you'll be cleaning up more messes.

Keep a chart of your new dog's elimination behavior for the first three or four days. Jot down what times she eats, sleeps, and eliminates. After several days a pattern will emerge that can help you determine your pup's body rhythms. Most dogs tend to eliminate at fairly regular intervals. Once you know your new dog's natural rhythms, you'll be able to anticipate her needs and schedule appropriate potty outings.

Understanding the meanings of your dog's postures can also help you win the battle of the puddle. When your dog is getting ready to eliminate, she will display a specific set of postures. The sooner you can learn to read these signals, the cleaner your floor will stay.

A young puppy who feels the urge to eliminate may start to sniff the ground and walk in a circle. If the pup is very young, she may simply squat and go. All young puppies, male or female, squat to urinate. If you are housetraining a pup under 4 months of age, regardless of sex, watch for the beginnings of a squat as the signal to rush the pup to the potty area.

When a puppy is getting ready to defecate, she may run urgently back and forth or turn in a circle while sniffing or starting to squat. If defecation is imminent, the pup's anus may protrude or open slightly. When she starts to go, the pup will squat and hunch her back, her tail sticking straight out behind. There is no mistaking this posture; nothing else looks like this. If your pup takes this position, take her to her potty area. Hurry! You may have to carry her to get there in time.

A young puppy won't have much time between feeling the urge and actually eliminating, so you'll have to be quick to note her postural clues and intercept your pup in time. Pups from 3 to 6 months have a few seconds more between the urge and the act than younger ones do. The older your pup, the more time you'll have to get her to the potty area after she begins the posture signals that alert you to her need.

Accidents Happen

If you see your pup about to eliminate somewhere other than the designated area, interrupt her immediately. Say "wait, wait, wait!" or clap your hands loudly to startle her into stopping. Carry the pup, if she's still small enough, or take her

It's not fair to expect very young puppies to be able to control themselves the way adult dogs can.

collar and lead her to the correct area. Once your dog is in the potty area, give her the command to eliminate. Use a friendly voice for the command, then wait patiently for her to produce. The pup may be tense because you've just startled her and may have to relax a bit before she's able to eliminate. When she does her job, include the command word in the praise you give ("good potty").

The old-fashioned way of housetraining involved punishing a dog's mistakes even before she knew what she was supposed to do. Puppies were punished for breaking rules they didn't understand about functions they couldn't control. This was not fair. While your dog is new to housetraining, there is no need or excuse for punishing her mistakes. Your job is to take the dog to the potty area just before she needs to go, especially with pups under 3 months old. If you aren't watching your pup closely enough and she has an accident, don't punish the puppy for your failure to anticipate her needs. It's not the pup's fault; it's yours.

In any case, punishment is not an effective tool for housetraining most dogs. Many will react to punishment by hiding puddles and feces where you won't find them right away (like behind the couch or under the desk). This eventually may lead to punishment after the fact, which leads to more hiding, and so on.

Instead of punishing for mistakes, stay a step ahead of potty accidents by learning to anticipate your pup's needs. Accompany your dog to the designated potty area when she needs to go. Tell her what you want her to do and praise her when she goes. This will work wonders. Punishment won't be necessary if you are a good teacher.

What happens if you come upon a mess after the fact? Some trainers say a dog can't remember having eliminated, even a few moments after she has done so. This is not true. The fact is that urine and feces carry a dog's unique scent, which she (and every other dog) can instantly recognize. So, if you happen upon a potty mistake after the fact you can still use it to teach your dog.

But remember, no punishment! Spanking, hitting, shaking, or scaring a puppy for having a housetraining accident is confusing and counterproductive. Spend your energy instead on positive forms of teaching.

Take your pup and a paper towel to the mess. Point to the urine or feces and calmly tell your puppy, "no potty here." Then scoop or sop up the accident with the paper towel. Take the evidence and the pup to the approved potty area. Drop the mess on the ground and tell the dog, "good potty here," as if she had done the deed in the right place. If your pup sniffs at the evidence, praise her calmly. If the accident happened very recently your dog may not have to go yet, but wait with her a few minutes anyway. If she eliminates, praise her. Afterwards, go finish cleaning up the mess.

Soon the puppy will understand that there is a place where you are pleased about elimination and other places where you are not. Praising for elimination in the approved place will help your pup remember the rules.

Scheduling Basics

With a new puppy in the home, don't be surprised if your rising time is suddenly a little earlier than you've been accustomed to. Puppies have earned a reputation as very early risers. When your pup wakes you at the crack of dawn, you will have to get up and take her to her elimination spot. Be patient. When your dog is an adult, she may enjoy sleeping in as much as you do.

At the end of the chapter, you'll find a typical housetraining schedule for puppies aged 10 weeks to 6 months. (To find schedules for younger and older

Housetraining is a huge task, but it doesn't go on forever. Be patient and soon your dog will be reliable.

pups, and for adult dogs, visit this book's companion web site.) It's fine to adjust the rising times when using this schedule, but you should not adjust the intervals between feedings and potty outings unless your pup's behavior justifies a change. Your puppy can only meet your expectations in housetraining if you help her learn the rules.

The schedule for puppies is devised with the assumption that someone will be home most of the time with the pup. That would be the best scenario, of course, but is not always possible. You may be able to ease the problems of a latchkey pup by having a neighbor or friend look in on the pup at noon and take her to eliminate. A better solution might be hiring a pet sitter to drop by midday. A professional pet sitter will be knowledgeable about companion animals and can give your pup high-quality care and socialization. Some can even help train your pup in both potty manners and basic obedience. Ask your veterinarian and your dog-owning friends to recommend a good pet sitter.

If you must leave your pup alone during her early housetraining period, be sure to cover the entire floor of her corral with thick layers of overlapping newspaper. If you come home to messes in the puppy corral, just clean them up. Be patient—she's still a baby.

Use this schedule (and the ones on the companion web site) as a basic plan to help prevent housetraining accidents. Meanwhile, use your own powers of observation to discover how to best modify the basic schedule to fit your dog's unique needs. Each dog is an individual and will have her own rhythms, and each dog is reliable at a different age.

Schedule for Pups 10 Weeks to 6 Months

7:00 a.m.	Get up and take the puppy from her sleeping crate to her potty spot.
7:15	Clean up last night's messes, if any.
7:30	Food and fresh water.
7:45	Pick up the food bowl. Take the pup to her potty spot; wait and praise.
8:00	The pup plays around your feet while you have your breakfast.
9:00	Potty break (younger pups may not be able to wait this long).
9:15	Play and obedience practice.
10:00	Potty break.

10:15	The puppy is in her corral with safe toys to chew and play with.
11:30	Potty break (younger pups may not be able to wait this long).
11:45	Food and fresh water.
12:00 p.m.	Pick up the food bowl and take the pup to her potty spot.
12:15	The puppy is in her corral with safe toys to chew and play with.
1:00	Potty break (younger pups may not be able to wait this long).
1:15	Put the pup on a leash and take her around the house with you.
3:30	Potty break (younger pups may not be able to wait this long).
3:45	Put the pup in her corral with safe toys and chews for solitary play and/or a nap.
4:45	Potty break.
5:00	Food and fresh water.
5:15	Potty break.
5:30	The pup may play nearby (either leashed or in her corral) while you prepare your evening meal.
7:00	Potty break.
7:15	Leashed or closely watched, the pup may play and socialize with family and visitors.
9:15	Potty break (younger pups may not be able to wait this long).
10:45	Last chance to potty.
11:00	Put the pup to bed in her crate for the night.

Appendix

Learning More About Your Beagle

Some Good Books

About Beagles

McCullough, Susan, *Beagles For Dummies,* John Wiley & Sons, 2006.

Musladin, Judith M., Anton C. Musladin, and Ada T. Lueke, *The New Beagle,* Howell Book House, 1998.

Smith, Carl E., *Basset Hounds and Beagles—With Descriptive and Historical Sketches on Each Breed, Their Breeding, and Use as a Sporting Dog,* Vintage Dog Books, 2006.

About Health Care

Eldredge, Debra M., DVM, Liisa D. Carlson, DVM, Delbert G. Carlson, DVM, and James M. Giffin, MD, *Dog Owner's Home Veterinary Handbook,* 4th edition, Howell Book House, 2007.

Hourdebaigt, Jean-Pierre, LMT, *Canine Massage,* Dogwise Publishing, 2003.

Pitcairn, Richard H., DVM, PhD, and Susan Hubble Pitcairn, *Dr. Pitcairn's New Complete Guide to Natural Health for Dogs and Cats,* Rodale Books, 2005.

Wulff-Tilford, Mary L., and Gregory L. Tilford, *Herbs for Pets,* BowTie Press, 2001.

About Training

Donaldson, Jean, *The Culture Clash,* James & Kenneth Publishers, 1997.

Fisher, Dave, *Rabbit Hunting: Secrets of a Master Cottontail Hunter,* Creative Outdoors, 2004.

Morn, September, *Housetraining: Your Guide to a Happy Healthy Pet,* Howell Book House, 2006.
Palika, Liz, *How to Train Your Beagle,* TFH Publications, 2000.
Rugaas, Turid, *On Talking Terms with Dogs: Calming Signals,* Dogwise, 2005.

Magazines

AKC Gazette
260 Madison Ave.
New York, NY 10016
www.akc.org/pubs/index.cfm

Better Beagling
P.O. Box 8142
Essex, VT 05451
www.betrbeagle.com

Bloodlines
100 East Kilgore Rd.
Kalamazoo, MI 49002
www.ukcdogs.com

Dog Fancy
P.O. Box 37185
Boone, IA 50037-0185
www.dogfancy.com

Dog World
P.O. Box 37185
Boone, IA 50037-0185
www.dogworldmag.com

Popular Dogs: Beagles
P.O. Box 37185
Boone, IA 50037-0185
www.dogchannel.com/dog-magazines/
popular-dogs/articlebeagles.aspx

DVDs

A Show Beagle Groomers Guide
This groomer's guide educates show exhibitors about how to present their Beagle in the show ring. Order it at www.geocities.com/beowulfny/links.html.

Clubs and Registries

National Beagle Club of America
Richard J. Nunez
1075 Route 82, Suite 10
Hopewell, NJ 12533
clubs.akc.org/NBC/
This is the national club for the breed; its web site has a great deal of information, including upcoming shows and competitions. There are also many all-breed, individual breed, canine sport, and other special-interest dog clubs across the country. The registries listed below can help you find clubs in your area.

American Kennel Club
260 Madison Ave.
New York, NY 10016
(212) 696-8200
www.akc.org

Canadian Kennel Club
200 Ronson Dr.
Etobicoke, Ontario
Canada M9W 5Z9

(800) 250-8040 or (416) 675-5511
www.ckc.ca

United Kennel Club
100 East Kilgore Rd.
Kalamazoo, MI 49002
(616) 343-9020
www.ukcdogs.com

Web Sites

All About Beagles

Beagles
www.beagles-beagles.com
This site provides general Beagle show and hunting information and links to other Beagle sites, including breeders and rescue sources.

Beagles on the Web
beagles-on-the-web.com
This site has information and resources for adopting or placing a Beagle throughout the United States and Canada.

BeagleSavvy.com
www.beaglesavvy.com
This Beagle blog from the U.K. has interesting articles about care, training, and news.

The Regal Beagle
http://members.aol.com/cokicola/beagle.htm
This aptly named site provides a wealth of articles and advice on caring for your Beagle. Written by a dog-loving Beagle owner, this web site will appeal to folks interested in delving slightly deeper into the world of Beagles.

Show Beagle
www.showbeagle.com
This site provides information about show Beagles through links to the National Beagle Club show, Beagle judges, a pedigree database, a breeder ring, books, and historical magazines.

Dog Sports and Activities

Canine Freestyle Federation
www.canine-freestyle.org
This site is devoted to canine freestyle—dancing with your dog. There's information about freestyle events, tips, and even music!

Delta Society
www.deltasociety.org
The Delta Society promotes the human-animal bond through pet-assisted therapy and other programs.

United Beagle Gundog Federation
www.ubgf.org
This national Beagle hunting club has its own 214-acre, fenced-in Beagle hunting site in Kentucky. The web site offers information about upcoming trials and the top ten field Beagles.

Canine Health

American Animal Hospital Association
www.healthypet.com
If you want to check out veterinary hospitals in your area, the American Animal Hospital Association web site provides a database of AAHA-accredited veterinary hospitals. The site also provides information about vaccinations, pain management, and parasite protection.

American Veterinary Medical Association
www.avma.org
The American Veterinary Medical Association web site has a wealth of information for dog owners, from disaster preparedness to both common and rare diseases affecting canines. There is also information on choosing the right dog and dog-bite prevention.

American Holistic Veterinary Medical Association

www.ahvma.org

If you're looking for a holistic veterinarian, the American Holistic Veterinary Medical Association has a database of veterinarians in your area. The site also provides information on holistic modalities.

General Information

American Society for the Prevention of Cruelty to Animals

www.aspca.org

The ASPCA web site provides advice on pet care, animal behavior, disaster preparedness, and is a resource for poison-related animal emergencies.

Infodog

www.infodog.com

This is a good site for locating AKC-licensed dog shows and obedience or agility trials in your area. It also provides links to rescue organizations nationwide.

Travel

Dog Friendly

www.dogfriendly.com

This web site publishes worldwide pet travel guides for dogs of all sizes and breeds. It includes information about dog-friendly events, attractions, resorts, vacation homes, and ski and beach locales throughout North America. Dog owners can benefit from the storm evacuation guide, tips on road trip preparation and travel etiquette, and even dog-friendly apartments.

Pets Welcome

www.petswelcome.com

Lists more than 25,000 hotels, B&Bs, ski resorts, campgrounds, and beaches that are pet-friendly. It even has listings you can download onto your GPS (global pooch system). The site supplies travel tips and blogs on travel recommendations for dog owners.

Index

Photo Credits:

Isabelle Francais: 11, 14, 16, 17, 25, 30, 33, 40, 43, 44, 45, 56, 57, 64, 66, 67, 69, 71, 74, 75, 82, 84, 95, 97, 101, 125, 126, 130, 132
jeanmfogle.com: 1, 4–5, 8–9, 12, 18, 19, 24, 26, 32, 35, 36, 41, 48, 49, 55, 59, 61, 72, 76, 86, 90, 93, 123, 133
Bonnie Nance: 22, 34, 38, 42–43, 53, 60, 87, 91, 94, 128
Tammy Raabe Rao/rubicat: 20, 29, 51, 52, 81, 102–103, 104